Riding the

WAVES

Contented Living in a Chaotic World

WAVES

GAYLE G. ROPER

BROADMAN
&HOLMAN
PUBLISHERS

Nashville, Tennessee

Published by Broadman & Holman Publishers, Nashville, Tennessee

Dewey Decimal Classification: 248
Subject Heading: CHRISTIAN WOMEN

Library of Congress Cataloging-in-Publication Data

Roper, Gayle G.
Riding the waves : contented living in a chaotic world / Gayle G. Roper.
p. cm.
ISBN 0–8054–2084–3 (pbk.)
1. Christian women—Religious life. 2. Contentment—Religious aspects—
Christianity. I. Title.
BV4527 .R65 2001
248.8'43—dc21
2001025494

1 2 3 4 5 6 7 8 9 10 05 04 03 02 01

Kristina —

The Lord bless you!

Gayle Roper

Col. 3:17

To Audrey
with thanks for all the years of keeping me
from drowning in a sea of papers and business stuff.
Now that you've left me,
I feel the paper tide creeping higher and higher.
But I forgive your leaving because the reason
is that wonderful third granddaughter
you and Chip have given us.
Go with God and my love.

Contents

Introduction

One of the first times I heard people use the phrase, "Be happy," was when I was in college and involved in sorority rushing.

"We just want you to be happy," was the phrase of choice whenever an upperclassman approached someone she was interested in pledging.

But what happens if you aren't selected by the sorority of your choice? Or any sorority? Or if you lose your job? Or if you contract a deadly illness? Or your spouse walks out on you? Or your child rebels and gets in terrible trouble? How can you be happy then?

Not that there's anything wrong with desiring to be happy. I admit freely to wanting that warm, cozy, all's-well-with-the-world feeling, and many times I've found it.

But many times I have not.

And I suspect the same is true of you. As the Scot and poet Robert Burns said, "The best laid plans of men oft go awry." Circumstances, illnesses, and disappointments all deflate that soaring hot air balloon we call happiness and send us streaking to the hard reality of earth, where we land in a heap and with a most decided *umph!*

My basic response to the umphs in my life was that there must be something better than happiness, something that outlasts circumstances. And I found to my delight that there is. God has offered us contentment.

Contentment may be conditional, as is happiness, but it can be long-lived, because its conditions revolve around our relationship with God who is constant instead of the felicity of our circumstances which vacillate wildly.

"I am not saying this because I am in need, for I have learned to be content whatever the circumstances" (Phil. 4:11 NIV). So how do we, like Paul, learn this wonderful life skill that is more stable and more God-derived than happiness? My prayer is that you will find answers to this question in *Riding the Waves*.

I extend much gratitude and many thanks to my professional friends who shared freely with me their thoughts on the various aspects of contentment: Randy Alcorn, Karen Ball, James Scott Bell, Lyn Cote, Athol Dickson, Sandra Byrd, Robin Jones Gunn, Patricia Hickman, Angela Elwell Hunt, Patricia Johnson, Lucy McGuire, Nancy Moser, Tracie Peterson, Deborah Raney, Francine Rivers, Georgia Shaffer, and Rachel Williams. Their responses are quoted throughout the book with their permission.

Your insights and wisdom never fail to amaze me. I count myself among the blessed to know you all. With resources like you to tap, how could I go wrong?

And to my friends at church—you guys have been wonderfully kind to share your lives and hearts so freely. You are those who make the body so encouraging and sustaining both to me and to all our readers.

My critique group and Prayer Board: in the nitty-gritty of writing, you folks make all the difference!

And, of course, to Chuck, who taught me about the angle of incidence equaling the angle of reflection: you are, as always, my rock and my love.

Chapter 1

Agree or Disagree?

One long-ago summer day our eight-year-old Chip did something long forgotten for which I felt compelled to discipline him.

"To your room," I said. "And don't come out until I say you can."

"But, Mom, the guys are waiting!"

And indeed they were, standing around like a small herd of young buffalo in the front yard.

"Then they'll just have to wait."

"But we've got plans!"

"Tough," I said, ever the understanding mother.

To hurry Chip on his way to the bedroom, I took him by the nape of the neck and escorted him down the hall to his bedroom. Naturally he resisted my gentle touch.

It was summer, and we were both in our bare feet, a fact I never considered when I began escort duty. It was a great surprise when I slammed my right foot into the back of his left heel. Children have very sturdy heels.

I'm not certain which Chip enjoyed most, his delay in getting to his room or my impromptu dance on one foot as I held the other. It was humiliating to find I'd broken my little toe in our collision.

Several years later I referred to this incident and was absolutely amazed when Chip said, "Oh, yeah. That's the time you kicked me."

"What? I never kicked you!"

"Sure you did. You broke your toe."

"I know I broke my toe, but not because I kicked you. I walked into the back of your heel."

"Sure, Mom. If that's what you say." Smirk, smirk.

"Don't you think that if I were going to kick you, which I'd *never* do, I'd be smart enough to aim for a more padded part of your anatomy?"

"Right, Mom. Right."

It's quite common for two people to see things differently and for each to think he or she has the right version. Ask any cop who has tried to get witnesses to agree on anything.

"The guy had long dark hair," says Witness One.

"No, he didn't. He had short dark hair," says Witness Two.

"What? Are you two blind?" says Witness Three. "He had blond hair cut just below his ears."

"Well, I know his shirt was blue plaid," says Witness One.

"Really?" says Witness Two. "I remember red."

"Come on," says Witness Three. "He was wearing a tan jacket."

Disagreement between individuals is also evident to any biographer trying to fit the conflicting memories of his subjects into an accurate whole.

"Then Joe said we should sue the pants off the doctors, so we did," says the biography's subject.

"Wait a minute," says Joe. "I never said anything of the sort. It was Uncle Louie who said that."

"Uncle Louie? Are you crazy? Uncle Louie was already dead by the time I had that accident. You told me to sue."

"Not me," says Joe. "I'd never say anything like that."

"Well, you said it, believe me."

"Did not."

"Did so."

"Well," says the biographer in a soothing voice. "We'll just say you chose to sue and forget where the idea came from, OK?"

Disagreeing with one another is a fact of life.

Sometimes we even disagree with ourselves. Opinions long held are abruptly open to internal debate because something has happened to cause us to look at a situation differently.

We may have read something that raised questions we hadn't previously considered. Or someone may have challenged us about a long-held belief or a seemingly invulnerable position like our stand on eternal security or the appropriateness of corporal punishment or the right of a mother to say, "Because I said so! That's why!"

As a result we find ourselves questioning what we had thought was a fixed conviction. Am I as naïve as he says because I believe in *sola fide*? Is voting a straight-party ticket really the sign of a stiff-necked, ill-informed individual? Am I old-fashioned and narrow-minded because I insist my kids dress up on Sundays?

Sometimes it's a trauma or a triumph that forces us to reevaluate our goals, ideals, and faith. We may begin struggling with how an adult's loss of a job or a child's serious learning disability fits into "all things work together for good" (Rom. 8:28 KJV). Or we may wrestle with how the blessing of a substantial raise or the fact that our unbelieving neighbors genuinely like us fits in with "everyone who wants to live a godly life in Christ Jesus will be persecuted" (2 Tim. 3:12).

I wrote the following piece because I suddenly felt uncertain about something as mundane as one of my favorite times of the year.

It's raining leaves, masses of them, and I'm feeling melancholy.

I often delight in the tumble of leaves from tree to ground, their spinning free fall seeming so alive, so invigorating.

Brisk fall days usually make me long to hold my face to the wind and feel its freedom blowing through my hair.

But today as I watch the yellow leaves whirl from the beech across the street, I don't see the beauty of the golden rain but the starkness of the tree left behind.

As our dogwoods shed their crimson foliage, I don't see the ruby deluge. I see the empty, lonely limbs, bare and ugly against the sky. I don't see the glory of autumn; I see only its death.

The brown leaves chasing one another down the street, falling over each other in their enthusiasm, depress me rather than delight me. The lone leaves struggling to remain on their branches seem engaged not in a valiant effort but a vain one.

I guess it's my perspective. I've heard some sad news today. A friend's husband is leaving her and their two babies. Another friend's child is rebelling dangerously. I see their fear in the empty reaching branches outside my window, their uncertainty in the passing of the warmth and sureness of summer.

Yet interestingly, the very passage of the season is a guarantee to my friends, to me, of God's constancy. The change is not

*radom happenstance. "Oh, dear, this year the leaves are falling."
No, it's purpose, it's plan, it's the Creator in control.*

And he's controlling our individual situations too. He's keeping watch over the number of hairs on our heads and the accumulation of hurts in our hearts. Through husbands' leaving, kids' rebelling, and leaves' falling, he's there, comforting, encouraging, and loving.

. . . God has said,
  "Never will I leave you,
    never will I forsake you."
So we say with confidence,
  "The Lord is my helper; I will not be afraid.
    What can man do to me?" (Heb. 13:5–6)

Sometimes we find ourselves disagreeing not only with others or with ourselves but with God himself. We find ourselves screaming, "Wait a minute, God. Something's not right here! This isn't what I signed on for!"

When I was twenty-six, I had a total hysterectomy for various health reasons. The surgery meant that I'd not only never menstruate again, not necessarily a bad thing; it also meant I'd never have children, definitely a bad thing.

"God, what are you doing here?" I asked. "This can't be right! You've made a terrible mistake! Chuck and I could make a wonderful baby. It would have his long legs and intelligence and my smile. I know the Bible says I should trust, and I do on one level. And I'm truly grateful that you've spared my life. But come on! This isn't fair!"

Now a man came up to Jesus and asked, "Teacher, what good thing must I do to get eternal life?"

"Why do you ask me about what is good?" Jesus replied. "There is only One who is good. If you want to enter life, obey the commandments."

"Which ones?" the man inquired.

Jesus replied, "'Do not murder, do not commit adultery, do not steal, do not give false testimony, honor your father and mother,' and 'love your neighbor as yourself.'"

"All these I have kept," the young man said. "What do I still lack?"

Jesus answered, "If you want to be perfect, go, sell your possessions and give to the poor, and you will have treasure in heaven. Then come, follow me."

When the young man heard this, he went away sad, because he had great wealth. (Matt. 19:16–22)

If disagreeing with people can get sticky and disagreeing with ourselves can get confusing, disagreeing with God can be downright dangerous to our spiritual and emotional development. And when we disagree with God, we invariably walk away sad, as did the young man.

I think I know what would have happened to the young man in the Bible if he had given away all his money and followed Jesus. It's the same thing that will happen to us when we agree with God and do as he says.

He (and we) would learn that all he (and we) need is found in God himself.

He (and we) would experience that wonderful certainty that God is more than adequate to care for him (and us).

He (and we) would realize that God would give him (and us) all that he (and we) need to survive the situation.

He (and we) would come to the point of *agreeing with God that he and what he has provided for us are sufficient for his purposes for us.*

We would find contentment.

Instead the young man fell prey to the enemies of contentment, and they are many. Perhaps for the young man, the problem was fear or maybe greed. Other enemies of contentment are envy and an ungrateful heart, regret and loneliness, disappointment and depression.

When hard things happen to us and we wonder what God's doing, it's not wrong to ask him what's going on. The danger is when we tell him it doesn't matter what he has planned; we want it our way, and we want it now!

"God, give me my job back! I've got kids to feed."

"God, how could you let my marriage crumble! I've done everything right. You know I have."

"God, how could you let my hands become so ugly with arthritis? You can't give me such pain! I'm the church organist, for Pete's sake."

"God, how come they have enough money to build that wonderful addition, and I can't even afford a coat of paint for my small, hated, and incredibly ugly living room? Where's fair here?"

"God, how come my kids have to commute to the local community college while hers go to that elite, prestigious school? We both know mine are smarter and more deserving."

"God, you can't take away my ability to have children! I want the experience of being pregnant, of bearing a child."

In our disagreements with God, we stand in danger of being like the sad young man who walked away from the very help he needed.

In this book we'll look at some of the ways disagreeing with God can show itself. We'll also consider our spiritual anchors—the character of God himself, obedience, godly choices, and spiritual commitment—so that we can ride, contented, on top of life's waves instead of drowning in chaos.

The goal of this book is to make our fuzzy and nebulous concepts of contentment practical and understandable. I want all of us to grasp the realities and ramifications of agreeing with God that he and what he has provided for us are sufficient for his purposes for us.

I want us all, by the grace of God, to find contentment.

QUESTIONS, QUESTIONS

1. When you were growing up, how did your family define *contentment,* either out loud or by example?

2. Is there an area in your life where you find yourself disagreeing with God about his provision for you? Or his provision for someone else?

3. *Webster's New World Dictionary* defines *contentment* as "being satisfied." From a natural, human point of view, is contentment possible? How does a Christian understanding of contentment differ from the world's?

4. Read Proverbs 19:23. What is necessary to rest content?

5. Does contentment produce passivity? Can contentment and ambition coexist? Contentment and progress? Contentment and dreams and goals?

Chapter 2

Definition: Contentment

*Agreeing with God that he and what he has provided for us
are sufficient for his purposes for us.*

I'm a New Jersey girl born and raised, and I've spent a lot of time
at the Jersey shore. When I was a child, my grandparents owned a
boarding house in Ocean City, New Jersey, and I was fortunate
enough to spend every July at their place. When I was in college, I
worked in Ocean City for four summers, meeting Chuck at the
Baptist church in town. (My parents also met in Ocean City back in
the thirties.) As young parents Chuck and I often took our kids to
Ocean City for vacations. I've used Ocean City as the model for fic-
titious town in several of my novels.

I love the shore because I'm fascinated by the ocean. Through the
years I've seen its many faces, and I could watch it for hours, whether

it's calm and gentle or hurricane-furious, spitting spume into the raging wind. Especially spellbinding to me is the sea at night with a waxing moon cutting a path right to my feet.

The waves heave and break, ebb and flow, rage and purr, but the shimmering moonlight always rides the pulsing swells directly to me. When I walk along the shore, the silvery sweep keeps step.

"The moon likes me best," I'll say to Chuck. "It comes right to me."

"Uh-uh," Chuck will say. "You just think it likes you best. But it's right here at my feet too. That's the way it works when the angle of incidence is equal to the angle of reflection."

Engineers are so romantic.

I don't understand the wonderful optical illusion that lays the moon at each person's feet, but I see it as a powerful illustration of the contentment we can know as God's women. Calamity and coincidence roil the surface of our lives, but the beam of God's contentment can ride the rocking tides right into our souls. We all stand at different spots in life, but the silvery swathe of God's peace runs directly into our hearts—if . . .

And there definitely is an *if.*

When the Lord gave the children of Israel the Law, he told them that the blessings he had for them were conditional.

"See, I am setting before you today a blessing and a curse—the blessing if you obey the commands of the LORD your God that I am giving you today; the curse if you disobey the commands of the LORD your God" (Deut. 11:26–28a).

The same conditional aspect of God's blessing applies today, not in the national sense it did for Israel, but in a personal sense.

"Do not be anxious about anything, but in everything, by prayer and petition, with thanksgiving, present your requests to God. And the peace of God, which transcends all understanding, will guard your hearts and your minds in Christ Jesus" (Phil. 4:6–7).

If we spend time with the Lord and tell him about everything, if we leave our worry and bring our thanks, we will find God's peace and contentment. Implicit is the idea that if we ignore God, we will find the world's confusion, chaos, and strife.

I don't know about you, but I want to ride on top of the waves, and I'm willing to spend time with God for the privilege. I want to seek him and find contentment.

In order to get a deeper grasp of how God's peace and contentment translate into our lives as women, let's look at the definition of *contentment* in three segments:

1. Agreeing with God
2. That he and what he has provided
3. Are sufficient for his purposes for us.

Agreeing with God

Whether we're watching a movie or reading a book, there's one sentence that's a guaranteed sign that the speaker is a bad guy. He takes the heroine by the hand, looks deeply into her eyes and says, "Trust me."

Don't do it, sweetheart, we think. *The guy's a rattlesnake.*

But of course she trusts him. She must if the movie is to last its requisite two hours or the story is to fill the blank pages between the covers.

A similar dynamic occurs when a teen wants to go to a party with questionable people. She looks at her parents with guileless, sincere eyes and says, "Don't you trust me?"

If the parent is smart, the answer is, "No. We don't trust anyone, including us, in the company of those guys."

Trust and assurance are only as good as the object of that confidence. The core of agreeing with God is found in the character and person of the God with whom we are agreeing.

Following the reign of Solomon, Israel was torn by civil war for many years. Finally the Northern Kingdom, made up of ten of the twelve tribes, fell to the Assyrians. The people were carried into captivity and gradually through the years assimilated into Assyria and the neighboring cultures.

The Southern Kingdom, made up of the tribes of Judah and Benjamin, was captured many years later by the Babylonians. Though carried into captivity, these two tribes were never absorbed; and after seventy years, they returned to their land in three separate migratory waves under the guidance of Zerubbabel, Ezra, and Nehemiah.

Their years in captivity had undermined the nation's already shaky faith, and the nationalists who returned to Israel were spiritually impoverished. The prophet Ezra began teaching them, and the people responded.

"Ezra opened the book [of the Law]. All the people could see him because he was standing above them; and as he opened it, the people all stood up. Ezra praised the LORD, the great God; and all the people lifted their hands and responded, 'Amen! Amen!' Then they bowed down and worshiped the LORD with their faces to the ground" (Neh. 8:5–6).

When all the people said Amen! Amen! they were agreeing with Ezra that what he said was true.

"We worship a great God!" shouted the prophet.

"You're right!" returned the people. "Amen! Amen! We agree. We worship a great God!"

Similarly, in the New Testament, Paul reminds us of who our God is:

Oh, the depths of the riches of the
    wisdom and knowledge of God!
How unsearchable his judgments,
    and his paths beyond tracing out!
"Who has known the mind of the Lord?
    Or who has been his counselor?"
"Who has ever given to God,
    that God should repay him?"
For from him and through him
    and to him are all things.
To him be the glory forever! Amen. (Rom. 11:33–36)

"We worship a great God," says Paul. "We can't begin to understand what he's thinking, nor can we repay him for what he has done. Everything—everything!—comes from him. Agreed? Agreed!"

There is also a future time when the great shouts of Amen! will ring.

"All the angels were standing around the throne and around the elders and the four living creatures. They fell down on their faces before the throne and worshiped God, saying: 'Amen! Praise and glory and wisdom and thanks and honor and power and strength be to our God for ever and ever. Amen!'" (Rev. 7:11–12).

Amen and amen!

THAT HE AND WHAT HE HAS PROVIDED

As I began thinking about *contentment,* I struggled to find a definition that was universal as opposed to American. If the meaning of the word were to be accurate in the light of the Bible, it had to be cross-cultural. After all, the Bible is for all people in all times in all places. I didn't want to fall into the American trap of assuming contentment meant abundance and success. I needed a definition that would work not only in our plenty but also in the Third World's poverty, in North Africa's drought, and in the political and financial chaos of the Confederation of Independent States.

One of my first conclusions was that happiness and contentment are two different things, one based on circumstance and the other based, as we have said, on God himself.

Several years ago, well before the fall of communism, writer Jerry Jenkins went to Romania on a fact-finding trip. He noted that the believers he met had not only "a deep joy but also a deep sense of sadness and frustration with daily life."

Jerry wrote, "I asked (a believer) if anyone but Christians were happy in his town. He struggled with the concept of happiness.

"'It is not an issue here,' he concluded. 'It's not attainable anyway.'"[1]

While happiness is a fine emotion, as these Romanians well knew, it is not always attainable.

I saw a picture in the *Philadelphia Inquirer* of a mother watching her teenage son being taken to jail for murder. The grief etched on that mom's face is an image I've never forgotten. No matter what happens in the future, this woman will never again know "happiness."

In contrast, joy and contentment come from knowing God on a level that allows total confidence in him. No matter what goes on, no matter the frustration, poverty, and emotional pain, God understands and is in control. It's this confidence in God's character that allowed the Romanian believers to live beyond their circumstances.

Chuck and I were privileged to be invited to the National Prayer Breakfast in Washington, D.C. a few years ago. Seated to my right was a Yugoslavian pastor named Peter. At the time, Yugoslavia had recently overthrown communism and was still one nation. Naïve Westerners like me assumed that American-style democracy and a strong capitalist economy were imminent.

"How was life for a pastor under communism?" I asked Peter.

"For me not too bad," he said. "Persecution had eased in recent years, even before the iron curtain parted. But my father, also a pastor, spent many years of his life in prison for the Lord. What concerns me now is the fear that my country is about to blow itself apart with civil war, and the freedoms we have gained will be lost."

Sadly Peter was correct. We read of the hatred between Bosnia and Serbia, and the malignancy of ethnic purging and centuries-old hatreds make daily headlines.

Why, when God was providing, did he put Peter, his family, and his congregation in the middle of a horrific civil war, another event in a long line of terrible events that have plagued that country? And why did he put me in a comfortable home in a country where we have political stability—"the majesty of the democratic system," George Bush called it in his 1992 concession speech.

I have no idea. All I know is the character of an all-wise God. Somehow in my life, Peter's life, and in the lives of the Romanian believers and that mother in Philadelphia, God is providing as he purposes.

ARE SUFFICIENT FOR HIS PURPOSES FOR US

Every Wednesday when I was in fifth and sixth grades, Mr. VanOss came to our house to give me piano lessons. When I began playing, I was very excited. I knew that shortly I would be running my fingers up and down the keyboard, making wonderful and very impressive music like my father did.

Then I learned about talent and practice.

As far as talent went, there seemed a good possibility that I might have some. My father was a professional musician, and genes will tell. However, it soon became obvious that while Dad had shared his love of solitude, his appreciation for history, his hazel eyes, and his upper lip with me, somehow his gift for music never made my DNA. And as for practice—I learned it wasn't any fun, especially when a dearth of talent was involved.

One day as Mom and I walked Mr. VanOss to the door, he looked at me, then at Mom. "I hate to say this, Mrs. Gordinier, but these lessons are a waste of my time, Gayle's time, and your money."

Thus ended my piano lessons. I imagine it was as much a relief to Mr. VanOss as it was to me.

Obviously being a professional musician or even a talented amateur was not what God had in mind for me. The truth was so obvious that I had no trouble accepting it.

It was harder to agree that when God removed my ability to have children, he was giving me sufficient for his purposes then too. My keen disappointment made endorsing God's plan more difficult—and more important.

Finally I accepted God's wisdom, and we adopted our two sons. It didn't take long to realize what God knew all along: my barrenness was sufficient for God's purposes, not only for me but for Chuck, and our adopted sons, Chip and Jeff as well.

Perhaps the vast differences in what appears to be God's sufficiency can be understood by the following illustration.

Two pilots are coming into two different airports. At one airport the runway lies clear and waiting in the sunlight. At the other the field is socked in with fog so dense that nothing is visible.

Both pilots call the tower for landing instructions. Both are told which runway to use, which approach to take, and when the way is clear for them to proceed with the landing. Both pilots drop to the ground, confident in the wisdom of the tower.

There's no question that the landing is less stressful for the pilot whose instructions are confirmed by his own eyesight. There's also no question that the pilot who can see nothing is totally dependent on the tower for his very survival. Contentment lives at the place where we are totally dependent on our Tower whether we can see where we are going or not, knowing and accepting that he will provide sufficient for his purposes for us.

"And God is able to make all grace abound to you, so that in all things at all times, having all that you need, you will abound in every good work" (2 Cor. 9:8).

QUESTIONS, QUESTIONS

1. When you think of God's character, what attributes enable you to agree with God that he knows what he's doing even when you don't?

2. Read Proverbs 3:5–6. What is one of the results of agreeing with God?

3. Read Psalm 13. Have you ever felt like the psalmist? What are we to do regardless of our circumstances?

4. Read James 1:17 and Philippians 4:19. What do these verses teach us? Have you ever felt like disagreeing with these verses?

5. Read 1 Thessalonians 4:3–6a. What are God's purposes for us according to these verses? Notice how cross-cultural these purposes are.

6. Are there instances in your life where God has allowed you to see his purposes clearly? How does this gift of insight affect the times when you can't see his reasons?

Chapter 3

Learning to Be Content

*God is most glorified in us when we are most
satisfied in Him.*
—John Piper, *The Pleasures of God*

One of the loveliest sights in God's great creation is sunlight
shimmering off a serene, blue lake. The dazzle temporarily blinds,
but we smile even as we blink. When a slight breeze ruffles the surface, these sun jewels dance gently for us, inviting us to celebrate
with them the wonder of our God.

Let's use these sparkling sun jewels as an illustration of all the
good days in our lives, the days when everything goes well and everyone smiles, when work gets finished satisfactorily, and people praise
our efforts. As it's easy to be delighted by the sun jewels, it's easy to
be contented on sun-jewel days.

In contrast, last night I stood on the dock at Sandy Cove Christian Conference Center in Maryland, looking at the black headwaters of the Chesapeake Bay. The night was very windy, and the water, already at high tide, was running before the wind. Small whitecaps stood out against the black water as it rushed and bucked. All was darkness and tempest.

All, that is, except for the white-gold avenue of molten moonlight that poured over the water directly to me. While the moon itself was only a waxing quarter, its pathway of radiance was strong and steady in spite of the blow.

I turned and looked in the other direction, away from the moon, and blackness instantly enveloped me. I could no longer see the waves, though I could hear them moaning and moving even above the rush of the wind. And I no longer had the comfort of the moon's glow.

When life's dark nights come, and we hear only wildness and chaos, and we see only blackness, it's hard to remember that contentment is even a possibility. Where is that golden light of God's comfort? Perhaps we cry, as did the psalmist, "How long must I wrestle with my thoughts and every day have sorrow in my heart?" (Ps. 13:2).

The steady beam is there, riding across the turmoil to us—if we're looking in the right direction. We have to *learn* to look not at the overwhelming darkness but at the constant ribbon of light. We have to *learn* to agree with God, to trust him with everything.

When Paul wrote to the Philippians, he talked about contentment. "I have *learned*," he wrote, "to be content whatever the circumstances" (4:11, italics mine).

I find this verse both fascinating and comforting. It's fascinating because it reconfirms the idea that contentment isn't automatic or easy. In fact, it frequently goes against our very natures. The verse is comforting because if the great apostle Paul had to learn to be content, then I shouldn't feel badly that I struggle with this concept, that I have to learn too.

I first found the concept of learning to be content when I was still in high school. I grew up in a delightful, loving family who cared for me deeply and well. My parents were wonderful, thoughtful people, but they had no interest in spiritual things. We never went to church. Sunday mornings were warm family times of breakfasts and reading the Sunday comics in the *Philadelphia Inquirer*.

When I was about eight, a new family moved in down the street from us, and they had a little girl my age.

"Do you want to come to Sunday school with me?" Margie asked.

I was one of those kids who are willing to try anything if it sounds like it might be fun. "Sure," I said, not realizing that I was about to change my life completely.

Sunday mornings became for me not a time of relaxing but of worshiping and learning. I found I enjoyed going to Sunday school, Vacation Bible School, and church, but in my mid-teens I also found myself resenting that I was always going alone. Church is a very family-oriented place, and if you come on your own, you have to latch onto other people to be your family. My friends' parents were very kind to me, welcoming me for a morning or an evening, but I began to get very embittered that my own family wasn't there with me.

I wish I could say I felt these emotions because I was worried about them spiritually. I'm afraid that my feelings were of a much more selfish nature. I didn't like being the proverbial square peg and feeling embarrassed as a result. I began to complain to the Lord.

"I'm always alone, Lord. I never feel like I fit in. I want Mom and Dad to come to church. Is that too much to ask?"

One morning during my devotions, I stumbled all unknowing on Philippians 4:11: "Not that I speak in respect of want: for I have learned, in whatsoever state I am, therewith to be content." (We always used King James in those days.)

The key word that leapt out at me was *learned*. If Paul could learn to be content with all that he went through—the stonings, the whippings, the shipwrecks, the asp bite, jail—so could I. After all, he and I worshiped the same God, and I had the same Holy Spirit he had. I would *learn* to be content going to church alone. Rather than get angry at my folks, expecting something from them they were unable to give, I needed to love them as the great people they were.

By the grace of God, I did learn to be content alone. It took lots of prayer, and I had to give up my need to be a "normal" part of the Body. I learned to accept what was, instead of what I wanted (though I, of course, still prayed for my family to become interested in spiritual issues). My resentment disappeared, replaced by genuine love and respect for Mom and Dad.

The second time the idea of learning to be content was a great challenge to me was when I found I would never be able to have children. "Whatever state I am in," the King James says, or whatever the circumstances. Again, my state was not of my choosing, but then neither was Paul's as he sat in jail writing about having sufficient. I thought of an old joke: I'll be content whatever state I'm in, but if the state's Hawaii, it'll be a lot easier.

Hawaii or Pennsylvania, there was a point in time when I had to agree with God that he knew what he was doing when he said, "No kids." And there have been countless times since then that I have had to remind myself of that decision I made to trust God.

You would think that now that I am well past childbearing age, my learning to be content, at least about this issue, would be easy.

Not so. There are times when it is still a struggle, believe it or not; times when I still have to remind myself of my commitment to agree with God.

This past summer I was watching my third granddaughter as she proudly took some of her first steps. Walking is hard work for a small one, and she was sticking her little jaw out as she fought for balance. I grinned at her because I sometimes stick my jaw out when I'm really concentrating.

Well, at least somebody looks a bit like me, I thought, and just like that, I felt a wash of tears because, actually, no one does look like me, and no one ever will. And I'm back to learning to agree with God that he's given me sufficient for his purposes, and in this situation sufficient is barrenness and no one looking like me.

We've talked about sun-jewel days and dark nights, but a climatic reality in Pennsylvania where I live now is the ice storm, intense washes of rain when the upper air temperatures are high enough to prevent snow, but the ground temps are cold enough to freeze the rain. The fascinating thing about the ice storm is that the driving rain and freezing temperatures often give way to a sunshot fairyland the next morning. Brilliant sunshine fills a crystalline blue sky and bathes the ice-encrusted landscape. Everything sparkles with an intensity that makes the eyes water. Trees backlit by the sun hold glowing arms to the heavens. Grass blades are frozen swords, and streets are rivers of ice, crisp and dangerous.

But it's our holly tree that's the true wonder, I think. Each ruby cluster of berries and each scalloped leaf are encased in a cocoon of ice. They shine with rare beauty, gems to the glory of God.

Then as temperatures rise, the melt begins. Drip, drip, drip. The tree trunks become sheets of liquid. The grass becomes pliable once again. The gutters become gushing rivers. Clumps of ice fall from the phone wires. Icicles lose their grip on the eaves and crash to the ground to shatter in myriad pieces. In short, it's life as usual.

There are times when we feel like we are the victims of an ice storm. We feel encased in ice but without any beauty to recommend the situation. All we see are the broken limbs and damaged landscape of our lives. How are we to trust in God when all around us is ruin? How are we to rest in the arms of the One who could have prevented our particular terror but didn't?

We survive the ice storms one faith step at a time, one small act of obedience and trust by one small act of obedience and trust. As the ice outside my window disappears one drop at a time, so contentment must be learned little by little. The more we choose to obey, the more we know contentment. Let me give you an example of how it works.

Jesus said, "Therefore I tell you, do not worry about your life" (Matt. 6:25a). Obedience means we mustn't worry. Now there's a chore, especially for some of us. I suspect we worry about different things, but each issue we're anxious over can become disobedience. It's the old Martin Luther quote about not being able to stop birds from flying over our heads but being able to keep them from roosting in our hair. Ideas to worry over come, threatening to rob us of contentment. Our choice is to shoo those birds away or to help them build their nests.

I have discovered that as I age, I could easily become a worrier of major proportions over the idea that men die before women. All I need to do is visit the retirement community where my mother-in-law lives to see the reality of that fact. The few men who are there are so popular it's funny.

The verse that says, "She can laugh at the days to come" (Prov. 31:25) has become harder for me to apply. What if Chuck dies and

I'm a widow? It's not that I'm afraid I couldn't manage without him. It's that I don't want to. The odds say, though, that this is what will happen. Augh!

Trust and obedience require that I not worry about the future. Contentment requires that I leave my possible widowhood in God's hands where it belongs. As drip by drip, obedience by obedience, I can learn contentment, in the same way, if I disobey and allow myself to become obsessed with the possibilities, drip by drip, disobedience by disobedience, I can learn discontent. So I must wave that particular bird away whenever it flies overhead.

Sun-jewel days, black midnights of pain, and ice storms that freeze our hearts—all must be left in God's hands where they belong if we are to learn contentment.

Some of our continuing struggle to rest in God's sufficiency is colored by our personalities as well as our thought processes. None of us will handle the learning to trust in exactly the same way or see the same reasons for developing this trust.

Let's set up a scenario and see how the different personalities might react to it. The following story is one that happened to me, and I'll tell you my way of dealing with it last.

Several years ago I went through a dry spell as a writer. I had had seven books published, and I thought I was on the way to establishing myself. Then suddenly, for five long years, I couldn't place a manuscript, book, or article anywhere. The only things that kept me going were occasional reprints of some articles previously published and my teaching at writer's conferences. Oh, yes, and a sense of a calling from God.

Near the end of that five years, I walked down to my mailbox one day and found two book manuscripts returned to me, rejected. Not one, which is devastating enough, but two! Let me tell all you non-writers that an immense amount of work and time went into those projects, to say nothing of my heart and soul. My emotional pain was intense.

I went up to the house and back to the bedroom. I climbed in bed and pulled the quilt up to my chin. I lay there staring at the ceiling, feeling very sorry for myself.

The cat jumped up on the bed and curled up in a ball in the angle between my neck and shoulder. He reached out and gently laid a paw on my cheek.

Well, I thought, *at least somebody loves me!*

And I began talking to the Lord.

Here's where the different personalities come in.

If I were a melancholy, intense personality, this is when I would have bemoaned my rejection as another proof that I wasn't good enough to be a real writer. I wasn't good enough to serve God.

"I tried my best, Lord," I'd cry. "I worked so hard to make everything perfect, but obviously it wasn't. I'll never be good enough. Never. I might as well give up."

I'd study my rejection letters and ponder what the I'm-sorry-we-can't-use-your-material-at-this-time really meant. I'd try to read between the lines between the lines. I'd analyze and internalize. I'd review my manuscripts and cringe at how bad they were. I'd be sorely tempted to put both projects in the bottom drawer and go to work as a greeter at Wal-Mart. After all, I deserve the darkness of chaos and disappointment instead of the light of contentment because of my imperfections. My vision for serving God would grow narrower and narrower until I concluded that he could never use me at all.

"Look outward," wrote Charles Krauthammer. "You have been rightly taught Socrates' dictum that the unexamined life is not worth living. I would add: The too-examined life is not worth living either."[1]

Mr. Krauthammer is right; the too-examined life is misery. How could it be otherwise when the one doing the examining and the self being examined are sinful? There's no perfection to be found, nor is there ever the possibility of perfection short of heaven. In order to be content, a melancholy temperament must learn to examine not herself and her world but the Father from whom comes all good and perfect gifts (James 1:17). She must change Mr. Krauthammer's quote from "look outward" to "look upward."

I'd like to suggest to all the melancholies lying on their backs, staring at the ceiling, coming close to hating themselves and their work that the answer is not giving up. Rather, it's pursuing excellence. Not perfection. Excellence.

"Whatever your hand finds to do, do it with all your might, for in the grave, where you are going, there is neither working nor planning nor knowledge nor wisdom" (Eccl. 9:10).

"Whatever you do, work at it with all your heart, as working for the Lord, not for men, since you know that you will receive an inheritance from the Lord as a reward. It is the Lord Christ you are serving" (Col. 3:23–24).

King Solomon, that wisest and wealthiest and most jaded of men, tells us to pursue excellence because when we die, we can't do anything more. True, but I like Paul's motive for excellence better. It's the Lord Christ we serve.

Notice that neither man says we should pursue perfection. We are to do things with all our might and with all our hearts. God does not expect perfection from us. That's what his grace is all about. That's why he offers forgiveness.

How does all this theory work for the melancholy woman mourning her lack of sales? Or struggling with being passed over for a promotion? Or dealing with rebellious teens? Or living with an unappreciative husband?

She must yield her need for perfection in her work and herself. She must accept God's call on her in spite of her imperfections. She needs to acknowledge God's right to use her as he sees fit with the product she can produce, the job she can perform, the mothering and wiving she can do, flawed as it all is.

> Do you not know?
>> Have you not heard?
> The LORD is the everlasting God,
>> the Creator of the ends of the earth.
> He will not grow tired or weary,
>> and his understanding no one can fathom.
> He gives strength to the weary
>> and increases the power of the weak. (Isa. 40:28–29)

God understands a sense of failure or even outright failure itself, and because he does, he gives strength and power. I don't understand how he does this. In fact, it's sort of mystical. I just know he makes up for our lacks when we ask him. He also makes our spirits to rest, to be content, when we yield our imperfections to him.

"A call for excellence is something I really believe in," writes novelist Angela Elwell Hunt. "I think it'd be sinful to offer God less than my best—but my best may not always be the most popular or the best-selling or marketable or whatever. Contentment then rides hand in hand with trust, because I've got to trust God that my books that are reaching people are touching people."

"Father God," our perfect melancholy learns to say, "I offer this manuscript (or whatever) to you. I've done my best, and while it's good, it still lacks. I just can't make it any better. Please make up for my inabilities. Use it in spite of me and my limitations. It's my gift to you. I rest content in you and what you will do with it."

If I were a phlegmatic, easygoing, peace-loving person lying there in the bed with my rejected manuscripts lying on the quilt beside me and the cat purring in my ear, my struggle would be different. Unlike my melancholy friend who knew deep down she deserved the rejection because she wasn't good enough, I'd be resentful of the disruption this day's mail brought me. Because I like everything to be without stress, I'd look at the returned book as an emotional snake sent to sink its fangs into me, and I'd want no part of it.

Since I hate anything that ruffles the calm of my life, I'd give very serious thought to getting out of the writing profession. I wouldn't want to deal with all the emotions that flare like an infected tooth when a piece written with my heart's blood is unappreciated, or when an editor sends a form rejection instead of a handwritten note, or when someone else publishes a piece about the very thing I'm writing on, beating me to it. Or when my husband is always after me to keep a tighter budget. Or when my next-door neighbor complains about my kids. Or when my boss picks at me over things that are so petty I can't believe he cares about them. I'll just ignore it all.

"Lord, this rejection (complaining, picking) is shattering my peace! I'm not writing so my life can be interrupted, you know. I just want to write and see my pieces get published. I don't want to weep over them. I don't want to deal with rejection. All I want is peace and quiet and the chance to serve you. I didn't sign on for this chaos. I'll just be content with not being published." Or not having a budget. Or not getting along with the neighbors. Or not pleasing my boss.

The phlegmatic individual's theme verse might be, "A heart at peace gives life to the body" (Prov. 14:30) because she seeks peace at almost any cost. She endures her teen's disrespect rather than fight for proper consideration. She won't confront her husband about his vulgar mouth because of the emotional stress such a showdown requires. She won't state her opinion because it might be divisive or she might have to defend it. She won't send the manuscript out again because it's not worth the tension and possible rejection.

The problem with this peace-seeking woman is that she may have equated contentment and peace with passivity, with taking the path of least resistance. She does not understand that agreeing with God and giving up are two very different things.

There is nothing quiescent about contentment. As novelist Angela Elwell Hunt points out, "Contentment carries a connotation of passivity; yet it's a very active struggle. It rides hand in hand with trusting God."

There is a price to be paid for every struggle, every achievement, spiritual or otherwise, and we must expect to pay it. This cost has nothing to do with God's love or lack of love and everything to do with living in a sinful world where everything has price tags. The phlegmatic individual must be willing to foot the bill even though it shakes up her vision of a peaceful little world.

The phlegmatic learns to pray, "Lord, you know how I get all tight inside when I have to struggle with something. I just want things to be peaceful, and I tend to draw back when I think the price tag of life is too steep. I know though that I have to be willing to pay the price in emotions and effort if I want to follow what I perceive to be your call on my life. By your grace, I will resubmit the manuscripts (or confront my teen or talk to my husband or tell the committee what I think) and wait upon you instead of withdrawing."

Different still is the sanguine, outgoing, bubbly person who likes to have fun in life. When she lies in the bed with the rejected manuscripts, she ends up playing with the cat. It's more fun to tease a pet than analyze what went wrong and be miserable. Her heart's cry is, "Lord, I just wanted to do something I enjoyed and help people at the same time. I didn't sign on to cry in disappointment, to have my guts wrung out with rejection. I don't like being left out of the publishing party. If it's going to be this rough, maybe I need to find something to do that's easier and more fun. I just want to be happy. Is that too much to ask?"

Our sanguine friend has to learn that having fun and being happy are not suitable goals for life. That's not to say that having fun and being happy are bad or evil. Certainly they aren't. We all like to laugh and enjoy. We all like to be happy. But if having fun or being happy becomes our objective, then we have chosen the lesser by far.

A sanguine individual has an advantage when looking for contentment because she tends to see the world as a place of great potential. She sees a half-full glass instead of a half-empty one. She wants to smile, wants to trust people. She sees no reason why people won't like her. It's a natural extrapolation that she thinks her book (or her phone call or her invitation to lunch or her new proposal at work) will be received gladly.

But what happens when the party is cancelled, the book not published, the new proposal rejected? Here is where the fun lover meets reality. Here is where the sanguine learns the difference between happiness and joy, between fun and contentment. Happiness and fun are rooted in circumstances. If all goes well, we experience them. These are our sun-jewel times.

In contrast, joy and contentment can be found in the blackest of nights—if our focus is on God, if, as novelist Robin Jones Gunn says, "Our perspective is on eternity instead of the ups and downs of life." The psalmist reminded us of this need to focus on the eternal.

Then will I go to the altar of God,
to God, my joy and my delight.
I will praise you with the harp,
O God, my God.
Why are you downcast, O my soul?
Why so disturbed within me?
Put your hope in God,
for I will yet praise him,
my Savior and my God." (Ps. 43:4–5)

The sanguine woman needs to learn to pray, "Lord, it's not fun being rejected like this (or having my brilliant idea ignored at work or my lunch invitation turned down or my phone call rebuffed). I don't like it. But, Father, I want you to be my joy and my delight. I want your contentment above happiness. If I go through some disappointments, I'll be fine because you are there to teach me what is best for me, to guide me, to give me peace like a river. I'm going to send these manuscripts out again, risking more unhappiness, because I believe it's what you want me to do."

And then there are choleric, controlling people like me who like to be in charge of every situation. In fact, when we aren't in control, we get nervous and frustrated. We tend to be ambitious, competitive, and achievement-oriented. Illnesses, loss of jobs, deaths, and rebellious children are difficult for us because of the lack of control we experience in each of those circumstances. Certainly my pair of rejected manuscripts indicated lack of control. Those editors made a choice without consulting me!

As I lay on my bed staring at the ceiling with the cat providing my only comfort as he purred in my ear, it was the reality of my helplessness that was so painful to me. Sure, I disliked not being seen as good enough, but even more I disliked my inability to make the editors change their minds.

"Lord, I wrote these for you. You know I did. Well, there was a little ambition and pride in there, but I doubt I can get away from the mixed motives as long as I'm a human being. Well, maybe there was a lot of ambition and pride, but the majority of my purpose was to honor you. You know it was. So what's with the rejections? With the five years of rejections?"

"I'm teaching you to let go," the Lord whispered. "I'm teaching you to agree with whatever I choose for you. I'm teaching you to be content whatever the circumstances."

"Oh, Lord, do you really have to? I'll still love you even if I'm a best-seller (or in charge of the drama team or CEO of my own company or setting the best-looking table of anyone in our dinner club). I promise."

But when God withholds success or good health or marriage or any of a number of things from those of us who like to call the shots, he breaks us. And we're forced to let go of whatever we desire so desperately. I had to trust my creations to the Lord because I could do nothing beyond write the best books I knew how. I was forced to let go of ambition in favor of God's plan.

"But seek first his kingdom and his righteousness, and all these things will be given to you as well" (Matt. 6:33). The difficulty for choleric people like me is that we want to define *all these things*. Yielding that authority to God is a hard thing, and it forces me to my knees time and again.

"I'm sometimes torn between two poles—ambition and vision," says novelist Patricia Hickman. "Ambition makes me feel anxious, makes my work feel forced, and pulls me away from the spiritual balance and regularity of a day found in God's ebb and flow. Vision for my work and my spiritual walk is birthed of God and his Holy Spirit. When I'm walking in God's vision for my work, I feel balanced, humble, steady, and obedient. I spend time with him and make him the firstfruits of my day. He pours himself into me when I open up my little, whiny mouth (I think of a baby bird) and say, 'I'm your vessel. Where next?'"

I think one of the reasons God withholds from us choleric control lovers is to remind us that we are merely earthen vessels—chipped, dinged, and lopsided. We're not as wonderful as we like to think. When we finally do achieve, we and everyone else know that it is all of the Lord. Novelist Nancy Moser notes, "Kneeling at the feet of our Lord, I know he will *not* say, 'I'm most proud of you for that book you wrote and the times you said, "I can do it, Lord!"' Not our Jesus. He'll cut to the chase: 'I'm most proud of you for those times you said, "I can't—but you can, dear Lord."'"

I eventually came to pray, "Lord, these manuscripts (or whatever) are yours. You know my heart's wish for them, but not my will but yours be done. I give up control to you."

So the manuscripts went out again, eventually finding publishing homes, but only after I learned valuable lessons about trusting God and being content with what he provides and when he provides it.

As I've thought about the learning process in relationship to contentment, I see two things we have to keep in mind to help us avoid frustration: time and tenacity.

It takes time to learn something. Simple sums must come well before advanced algebra or calculus. This summer our granddaughter Abby tripped over her feet, but eventually she'll run with the rest of the kids.

During my college summers I worked as a waitress in Ocean City, New Jersey. In the process I learned to carry three plates on one arm, four if really pressed. I learned to put the pie on the table with the point toward the customer and the coffee cup with the handle angled for easy lifting. I learned to serve from the right and clear from the left. I learned to carry a large tray full of food balanced on one hand. I learned to smile no matter how cranky the customer.

But I didn't learn all these skills at once. Oh, I got the head wisdom easily enough but not the practice. While I knew where to place the plates on my arm to carry them, I could only learn to balance them properly through experience. The first time I tried two plates on the same arm, I trailed *au jus* from a prime rib dinner all the way from the kitchen to the table, arriving with no *jus* left, a brown stain running down my uniform skirt, and an unhappy worker following me, mopping up. In the process of learning to handle a filled tray, I lost more than one before I got the feel for managing and distributing the weight.

But by continuing to work at it, I got to be very agile, developing to the place where spilling or dropping was a very rare thing. All I needed was enough time to practice and enough tenacity to hang on until I got it right, until I became proficient.

Learning to be content is much the same in that it takes time and tenacity to develop the spiritual discipline of agreeing with God. In every life new challenges constantly test our willingness to trust that God knows what he's doing. We shouldn't expect to know contentment at the click of our spiritual fingers any more than we should expect to have a full-orbed prayer life without practice.

The writer of Hebrews speaks of the mature believers who by constant use have trained themselves to distinguish good from evil. In other words, they practiced until they could tell the difference between right and wrong, not always an easy task in any age. Gray areas abound, and it takes time and tenacity to discern.

"So, Gayle," you ask. "Are you saying that the secret of contentment is simply time and tenacity?"

No. Time and tenacity allow us to learn the spiritual discipline of contentment, reminding us that spiritual growth doesn't happen in the twinkling of an eye. But the secret of contentment is far more powerful.

"I know what it is to be in need," Paul writes, "and I know what it is to have plenty. *I have learned the secret* of being content in any and every situation, whether well fed or hungry, whether living in plenty or in want. I can do everything *through him who gives me strength*" (Phil. 4:12–13, italics mine).

The secret of being content is, quite simply, him who gives me strength.

"My contentment," says novelist Francine Rivers, "is completely, utterly centered in Christ. When I turn my focus away, I may be entertained, titillated, distracted. But when I'm living by my own will, I'm not content. I'm not at peace. Everything Scripture has to say about contentment is summed up as follows, at least for me: Hear, O Israel: The LORD our God, the LORD is one. Love the LORD your God with all your heart and with all your soul and with all your strength (Deut. 6:4–5)."

It's through him that we find strength to do everything he asks of us. It's in him that we abide, resting safe through the gales of life. It's from him that we receive all we have, whether bounty or scarcity.

And it's by his strength that we learn to agree with God that he and what he has provided are sufficient for his purposes for us.

QUESTIONS, QUESTIONS

1. When Paul says he can do everything through Christ who strengthens him (Phil. 4:13), how do you think he defined *everything?*
2. Read Psalm 119:71. Do you agree with the psalmist's conclusion? Why or why not?
3. Read 1 Peter 3:8–10. What are we to learn to do, and what are the benefits if we learn?
4. Read Hebrews 13:5–6. What does the writer feel is the greatest value? The least value? How does it fit with Philippians 4:12–13?
5. What areas of your life can you identify as arenas in which you need to learn to be content?

Chapter 4

Despair

*I never understood why when you died, you didn't just vanish,
and everything could just keep going the way it was only you
just wouldn't be there. I always thought I would like my
tombstone to be blank. No epitaph and no name.
Well, actually I'd like it to say figment.*

—Andy Warhol

The above quote from artist and pop icon Andy Warhol is fascinating and scary in what it reveals of his psyche. He'd like his tombstone to say figment? He'd like people to think he wasn't real? That
they only thought him? That there was nothing more to him than
what someone's imagination conjured up?

Another time Warhol said, "The interviewer should just tell me
the words he wants me to say and I'll repeat them after him. I think

41

that would be so great because I'm so empty I just can't think of anything to say."[1] He also said, "If you want to know Andy Warhol, just look at the surface of my paintings and films and me, and there I am. There's nothing behind it."[2]

I'm so empty. Just look at the surface. Figment.

These words of Andy Warhol are very sad words to me—the words of a despairing, hopeless man, a man with no connection to the living reality that is God. Since Warhol never made any claim to faith, I shouldn't be so surprised that he felt empty and unreal.

But lots of times those of us who are Christians pass through seasons of despair too. There are many reasons for our descent into despondency, and I'd like to look at some of them and then discuss why we can respond differently from people like Warhol who are without the hope of Christ.

Some fall into despair because they feel *trapped.* Their circumstances at home or on their job or even in their church overwhelm them. They see problems on every side, but they see no way out.

Joe was the pastor of a dying church, one that was killing itself with internal strife. He was aware that the church had problems when he came, but he was confident God would give him the wisdom and courage to straighten things out. He and his wife, Melanie, agreed that by the grace of God they would pull this church back from the brink of self-destruction.

It took little time to see the futility of that dream, and after three very long years leading the church, Joe and Melanie saw no positive changes. If anything, the death knell for the congregation rang more loudly than ever.

"I can't stand it much longer," Melanie said as she sat in my living room crying. "The old ladies are constantly criticizing Joe. He can't do anything right. Well, I can't either, but it's Joe they go after. It seems every day someone flays him alive. 'I don't mean to criticize, but . . .' No matter what kind of message he preaches, it's the wrong kind. No matter how many people he visits, it isn't enough.

"If he talks to Mrs. Spencer and her cronies, somehow Mrs. Warrington and her friends hear about it and won't speak to him, at least not face to face. They get on the phone and tell everyone they can reach about how disappointed they are in Joe, and since God isn't blessing the church, it must be Joe's fault. Maybe he should leave.

"If he talks to Mrs. Warrington, Mrs. Spencer is in his office first thing the next morning to tell him he's letting the ungodly faction drag him down. 'Don't listen to that woman! Don't listen!' If Joe were truly the man of God he claimed to be, she says, he'd understand the problems Mrs. Warrington creates and avoid her.

"And then there's the Hammond family who won't even go out the church front door on Sunday mornings because they might have to shake Joe's hand. That's because once Joe preached against pride, and Mr. Hammond knew Joe was talking about him and holding him up to ridicule."

I blinked. "How did he know that?"

Melanie looked forlorn. "Don't ask me. I'm only the pastor's wife."

"How's Joe holding up under all this pettiness?" I asked.

Melanie shrugged. "He's doing better than I am. He still thinks God has called us here and won't think of leaving. I, on the other hand, am constantly pleading with God to get us out of here! I'm feeling so depressed that I don't know what to do. I sit around and cry all day. I feel like God has let us down."

That Melanie felt trapped is an understatement.

Unrealized expectations also plagued Melanie, and they too can eat at a person until despair takes hold. I saw this happen to Mac, a single man who went to the mission field with great expectations and high hopes. He worked with an unreached people group in a remote part of a South American jungle.

"When they hear the Word, they'll respond to the Lord with thanksgiving and in great numbers. I just know it. I've got the best ideas and plans!" Since everything Mac had turned his hand to up to this point had prospered, he had no reason to expect otherwise.

But Mac's people didn't respond to him. They barely tolerated his presence, and Mac, a gregarious person who needed friends and people to talk with, became more and more despondent. The heat, the bugs, and the difficulties with getting decent food made a troublesome situation even more so, but it was the solitude and the people's indifference that undid him.

"God, what am I doing wrong?" he'd ask day after day, night after night as the villagers went about their business as if he were invisible. "I thought you wanted all men to come to you! Why aren't they responding? Why aren't you answering my prayers? Where are you, God?"

Mac came home midterm, a broken and changed man. He felt a failure, deserted by God. He knew he had disappointed all those who had supported him financially and in prayer. Well, they couldn't be any more disappointed in him than he was in himself. None of his great dreams and plans for God had come to pass.

He tried to understand what had happened. Maybe God didn't care about his people, but how could that be true when he loved the world enough to send his Son? Then it must be that God was not listening to him. Yes, that must be it. He was the problem. He had done something that offended God so much he wouldn't listen. But what could it be? And hadn't God told believers in his Word to come boldly to the throne of grace? Mac went over and over his actions, motives, and thoughts.

The more Mac struggled to find answers that he could live with, the more depressed he became.

Shirked responsibilities can lead to despair as the consequences of the shirked duties pile up.

Annabelle had four little ones, all under four, the youngest a set of twins. The chaos at home began when she was nursing the newborn twins and never getting a full night's rest. Because of her weariness, jobs she had previously been able to keep up with began to be ignored. The vacuuming seemed unimportant when she'd had less than four hours sleep a night for the last five weeks. The dishes began to pile up when potty training the middle child became a necessity. Going to Wednesday morning Bible study was out of the question when it came time to get all four babies in winter gear. And why pick up the toys that were scattered all over the floor when they would just be dragged out again tomorrow?

Before Annabelle knew what was happening, she was so depressed she could barely function. She sat on the sofa or lay in bed most of the day, moving only when a child screamed for her. She fell into mothering by crisis.

"It's postpartum," everyone said, and at first she agreed, even though she'd had no problems of that nature with the first two children.

One day as she schlepped around in the same sweatsuit she'd worn for the past three days in spite of the sour milk smell and the food stain on the chest, it dawned on her that every time she looked in the laundry room and saw the mess, she flinched emotionally. And every time she glanced in the living room and saw the toys and clutter and half-eaten food, she sank lower. And every time she looked at herself in the mirror, she panicked. And when she tried to remember when she'd last talked to her husband or to God without complaining, she couldn't.

It's not postpartum, she thought. *It's me!* And she was right.

The *loss of a loved one* can cause despair to envelop you.

I watched what grief did to my mother. When Dad died, Mom did not cope well, much to my surprise. She had always been a model to me of all that a woman could be, and this well before women's rights and feminism flowered in the seventies. She'd lettered in sports back in the twenties, had a job and married in the thirties. She had her children in the forties, one before the war and two after. She started a business out of our home in the fifties. She went back to college in the sixties, having only completed one semester as a young woman before my grandfather lost everything in the crash of '29. She taught special ed in the seventies and cared for my father through the eighties as his health deteriorated.

When I was growing up, she often told me, "If you can do as well as or better than the boys, do it, Gayle. Don't be coy or cutesy."

As a result I never considered being female a hindrance. I also didn't have many dates in high school, but that's another story.

I expected that this strength of character would see Mom through the pain of Dad's death. Not so. My brothers and I were floored when she took to sitting in her favorite chair and staring at my father's picture all day.

"Mom, you've got to get out," we'd say. "Why don't you volunteer at the library or the hospital?"

She'd seem to consider the suggestions, but she did nothing about any of them. Rather she sat and stared.

One time, in an effort to bring her out of the emotional fog that was wrapping itself ever more tightly about her, my brother removed Dad's picture from the desk where it sat. She was furious at him. It was the one time she showed any genuine emotion except apathy in the five years she lived beyond my dad. In the end, despair claimed her, and even we kids and grandkids didn't give her reason enough to live. Her doctor actually put on her death certificate as the cause of death: lack of will to live.

There are also *physical causes* for despair. Tendencies to deep melancholia may be carried in a person's DNA, and illnesses like manic depression are genetic conditions as much as cystic fibrosis or sickle-cell anemia. The overwhelming despair termed *clinical depression* has its roots in the body. Also head injuries may cause a change in personality with resulting depression. We watched this happen to a very positive, choleric friend of ours who, following an accident, became despairing and uncertain.

My husband, Chuck, suffers from hypoglycemia, a blood sugar condition that can cause anxiety, nervousness, wakefulness, sweats, and various other symptoms. The stress of graduate school brought the latent illness to the surface, but it was years before we realized that his symptoms were actually related to disease.

Since one of Chuck's most obvious symptoms was anxiety, it was easy for him to conclude that he had a spiritual problem. After all, doesn't Scripture say, "Be anxious for nothing" (Phil. 4:6 KJV)? In this instance the difficulty with assuming a spiritual problem was that Chuck was a most consistent and godly man. I lived with him; I knew he practiced what he preached.

Finally, after twelve years of anxiety and wondering, we found a Christian counselor who was wise enough to send Chuck for a complete physical workup before he began the counseling. And boom!

There was the blood sugar problem. What Chuck needed wasn't spiritual correction (at least no more than any of the rest of us) but dietary changes. Cut the sugar and increase the protein, and he felt like a new man.

But it's not always that easy, not by a long shot. Writer Robert Benson faced true physically caused depression.

"I thought I was losing my mind, and it turns out that I was not too far off the mark . . . When Norma (a hospital worker) came to take me away, I figured I was being taken away for good, that I was likely to spend the rest of my life in a padded room trying to make sense of the task of tying my shoes. Later in the day, they came and took my shoestrings away from me, along with my belt, my pocketknife, my car keys, and my shoes. I remember being relieved. They were afraid I might hurt myself with them; I was afraid I would never be able to figure out which of the three drawers in my room to put them in."[3]

Our dear friend and pastor Rick Rodriguez calls himself a depressive personality. Over the years we've known him, we've seen him swim against the current of his own inclinations in his determination to honor God.

"Medication relieves the physical symptoms created by my chemistry imbalance, things like sleeplessness," Rick says. "While I'm holding my own, I take less than is prescribed. When I feel the blackness coming, I immediately up the dosage to the full amount. I also suffer chronic back pain, and the combination of depression and pain is a bad one."

Rick leaned back in his chair as we talked. "If I were to remain useful in ministry, which was my heart's desire, I knew I needed to learn to make proper decisions, godly decisions. I needed to learn discipline so I wouldn't reinforce the natural tendency of depressive persons to think differently from nondepressed people. Did you know that we think differently? We do. My natural thoughts can be counterproductive to my own good, to say nothing of counter to the Word of God."

"What do you mean, you think differently?" I asked.

"We obsess on things. We dwell on some tangential issue and make a big deal of it. I know that when I begin a downward cycle, one of the sure signs is that I begin to be overly concerned about unimportant things to the exclusion of what is truly important.

"For example, I remember years ago before I understood my tendencies that I became obsessed with the hangers on the coatracks around church. I'd go around straightening them, making certain they were all hooked the same direction and all an inch apart. Now I ask you, in the range of a pastor's duties, where do the hangers rate?

"Last year my wife came to my office and sat down. I know something's up when Eileen sits down, because she's a mover who never stays still. 'Richard (our twenty-year-old son) says that you're getting caught up in petty details,' she said. 'Is that true? And if it is, please do what you need to do.'

"I thought about Richard's observation, and I realized he was right. I was straying into the unimportant, a sure sign I was beginning a downward cycle. Immediately I upped my medicine and began to monitor my thinking. I was so thankful for the wisdom of my son and wife."

It's very important to realize that when you suffer from physically caused depression, mildly like Chuck or more seriously like Robert Benson and Pastor Rick, getting well/feeling content is probably not as simple as trusting God. Once in a while he performs a great healing miracle for a depressed person, but most times it's life as usual, emotional and mental struggles and all.

We've talked about some of the causes of despair—feeling trapped, having unrealized expectations, living with shirked responsibilities, dealing with the death of a loved one, having physical propensities in that direction. Chronic pain or health problems, the world situation, a business or church or marriage or parenting failure, and continuing guilt over a wrong done are more of the many causes of despair.

The thing that interests me about many of these causes is that they aren't wrong in and of themselves. There's nothing sinful about chronic health problems or great expectations. There's nothing wrong with mourning the death of a loved one or being distressed by failure. There can come a time, however, when the despondent person's *response* to despair becomes wrong.

We all understand Melanie's distress at the church situation she and Joe face. It's her doubting God that will lead her into trouble.

With Mac, our disappointed missionary, his sorrow at the lack of response from the people he'd hoped to help wins our sympathy, until we remember that he wanted them won in his pattern and on his schedule.

Of course my mother sorrowed deeply at my father's death. We expected nothing less. We did not foresee that she would place his memory above everyone and everything, including God.

And it's natural that Annabelle, our oh-so-weary mother, would be overwhelmed by her young charges and their care requirements. The wrong behavior came when she gave up even trying, letting chaos and crisis reign.

There is a tendency on the part of those who sympathize with the hurting depressive to relieve him or her of personal accountability in actions and thoughts. "They can't help it," we say. "It's not their fault. It's their circumstances, their illness, their upbringing."

But with self-discipline and the Lord's help they can and they must accept responsibility for themselves.

Hannah and Tom are both bipolar or manic-depressives. They have both had many manic episodes where they have gone for days without sleep, acting in bizarre, over-the-top ways. Both have visited the Slough of Despond several times and been tempted to harm themselves while there. Hannah has overdosed at least four times, and Tom has played very dangerous games with guns.

Hannah refuses to take her medicine or listen to her doctor and counselor. She continues to drink, take recreational drugs, and eat poorly. She is out of control, a danger to herself and a cause of heartbreak in her family.

Tom, on the other hand, has accepted accountability for himself. He eats well, takes his medicine, visits his counselor regularly, and has pursued a deeper walk with the Lord. He is back at his job and functioning well. He recognizes that it will all fall apart if he ever stops accepting personal responsibility for his actions, and he knows the strength for that discipline comes from his relationship with God.

No matter what the cause of the despair, the rock-bottom answer is the same: God. I don't mean that in any simplistic way, but what else is there when you get right down to it?

"It's important that you don't waste your sorrows," Pastor Rick says. "Our frailties are the means for his strength. I've had to learn disciplines to keep from being overwhelmed. Complete and utter dependence on God is my only way of retaining control."

Analyzing despair in enough depth to determine what is genuine distress and what has become a sinful response to distress is difficult. At a time when clear thinking is at best difficult and at worst almost impossible, there is a great need to think biblically. God has put us in community in the church for several reasons, and one of the primary reasons is to be of help to one another. When despair strikes, some women will be able to work their way through the emotions and the uncertainties on their own. Some would do well to talk with a wise friend or a counselor. Some will have families who will make all the difference, like Pastor Rick's wife.

"In the dark days when Christ came to me as I lay on my mat," writes Robert Benson, "on the day Christ said to me, 'Do you want to be healed?' it was Norma (the hospital worker) who kept saying yes, not me. I was too tired, too ill, too afraid, too uncertain, too ready to die. It was Norma and my sister and my friends and a couple of dozen strangers who took me to the Healer."[4]

It's tiring, draining, and just plain hard work to be the one who takes someone to the Healer when she is too weary or too confused to take herself. But what would have happened to the paralytic if his friends hadn't cared enough for him to go well beyond what people expected? What would have happened if they hadn't lugged his pallet up onto the roof, broken through the roof tiles, and lowered him to Jesus?

Someone has to hold us, take us to God when we're too weary. Someone has to call us on our excuses and turn our eyes back to God when we focus on how terrible our lives are. Always, always she must turn our eyes back to God. What a privilege when God calls you or me to be that one.

Mollie and I met at a local restaurant and took a table in a corner where we could have a modicum of privacy.

"What's up?" I asked as soon as we'd given our orders.

Mollie smiled her sweet smile. "I just need someone to share my thoughts with, someone to tell me if I'm nuts."

I watched Mollie as she spoke. She was a short, slim blond with round blue eyes and a sweet smile. "You may be many things, Mollie, but nuts isn't one of them."

"You know Ted pretty well, right?"

I nodded. Chuck and I had known Ted for several years, ever since he came to our church as a young man newly returned to the Lord. Chuck had encouraged Ted in his renewed faith, and we frequently had him in our home. We had watched his romance with Mollie with interest, and I had cried with joy at their wedding.

"You know Ted can be moody?"

I nodded, thinking that "moody" might be an understatement. Ted could be brutal if he chose. When we first knew him, he had had a razor-sharp tongue, but as he grew in his relationship with the Lord, the critical attitude diminished. Diminished, not disappeared. Mollie's charming, upbeat personality seemed to be just the thing he needed. Evidently Ted thought so too because he pursued her with great determination. At the time of our conversation, they had been married almost ten years and had three children, a boy and two girls.

"Is Ted giving you trouble?" I asked.

She shrugged. "No more than usual."

"Which means?"

"I thought we were doing pretty well," she said with a sigh. "Ted's a high-maintenance husband, wanting everything just so, expecting me to do whatever he wants. I knew that when I married him, though I didn't realize just how wearing his critical attitude would be."

I smiled sympathetically, thinking how glad I was that Chuck is so accommodating and adaptable. With me for a wife, he needs to be.

"We had a conversation last night," she continued. "He told me that in all the time we've been married, he thought we had maybe three good weeks."

I stared at her, appalled. "He actually said that?"

Mollie nodded. "He wasn't being nasty when he said it. At least he didn't think he was. He wasn't yelling or anything. In fact, he wasn't even mad about anything. He was just telling me what he thought."

I knew how devastated I'd be if Chuck ever told me anything like that, and I looked at her with renewed respect. Here she was sitting in a restaurant, eating lunch, and talking quite normally when she'd just been told something that would have rocked my world.

"What did you say?" I asked.

She shrugged. "I told him it hadn't been that bad for me, and I was sorry he was so disappointed." Then she spoke a spiritual truth that I had known before but never seen so clearly embraced. "I told him that I had learned early in our marriage that I wouldn't find my joy in him. He was too critical and judgmental. I was learning to find my joy in the Lord."

Many women in Mollie's situation would be in despair. Instead Mollie was learning "to find my joy in the Lord." She was learning what I call the Nevertheless Principle, which states that though things are bad, very bad, *nevertheless* we can trust in and depend on the Lord. This principle is stated again and again throughout Scripture.

One example is the prophet Jeremiah, a man who knew despair. Everything he did for the Lord seemed to backfire on him. He ended up rejected by the people he was sent to, his reputation in tatters. Men plotted to take his life, and he was commanded by God not to marry or have children. He was beaten and placed in the stocks, arrested several times, thrown in a cistern where he sank into the mud, and the words he had written were burned by his enemies. He wrote about how utterly betrayed and alone he felt.

Like a bear lying in wait,
    like a lion in hiding,
he [Jeremiah's enemy] dragged me from the path and
    mangled me
    and left me without help.
He drew his bow
    and made me the target for his arrows.
He pierced my heart
    with arrows from his quiver.
I became the laughingstock of all my people;
    they mock me in song all day long.
He has filled me with bitter herbs
    and sated me with gall.
He has broken my teeth with gravel;
    he has trampled me in the dust.
I have been deprived of peace;
    I have forgotten what prosperity is.
So I say, "My splendor is gone
    and all that I had hoped from the LORD."
I remember my affliction and my wandering,
    the bitterness and the gall.
I well remember them,
    and my soul is downcast within me. (Lam. 3:10–20)

These are the words of a man who knew deep emotional distress. I think the words that sadden me the most are when he says that he has lost all that he had hoped for from God. When God first called Jeremiah, he was young and reluctant. Even though God told him that he had been set apart from birth for the job he was being called to, Jeremiah said, "Ah, Sovereign LORD, . . . I do not know how to speak; I am only a child" (Jer. 1:6).

" 'Do not be afraid of them, for I am with you and will rescue you,' " declares the Lord" (Jer. 1:8).

"Then the Lord reached out his hand and touched Jeremiah's mouth and said, 'Now, I have put my words in your mouth. See, today I appoint you over nations and kingdoms to uproot and tear down, to destroy and overthrow, to build and to plant' " (Jer. 1:9–10).

I think if I were Jeremiah, even knowing the fate of many of the prophets of Israel, I'd have been pretty excited and overwhelmed. God was calling me for this special responsibility. And it just got better because God gave Jeremiah more assurances.

" 'Today I have made you a fortified city, an iron pillar and a bronze wall to stand against the whole land—against the kings of Judah, its officials, its priests and the people of the land. They will fight against you but will not overcome you, for I am with you and will rescue you,' declares the LORD" (Jer. 1:18–19).

And confident that God would make him a fortified city, an iron pillar, and a bronze wall, Jeremiah went forward, speaking faithfully all the words the Lord gave him. And he ended up years later writing of the intense emotional and spiritual pain when all he had hoped from the Lord was gone.

But here is where the Nevertheless Principle kicks in.

"Lord, my life is in ruins all about me, but . . ."

"Lord, everything is falling apart, nevertheless . . ."

"Lord, all I had hoped for from you is gone," Jeremiah wrote.

Yet this I call to mind
    and therefore I have hope:

Because of the LORD's great love we are not consumed,
  for his compassions never fail.
They are new every morning;
  great is your faithfulness.
I say to myself, "The LORD is my portion;
  therefore I will wait for him." (Lam. 3:21–24)

We want life to be pleasant. We want things to go well. We want to be happy. When things don't turn out this way, it's so easy to look at the despair we feel as the end of everything. It's only natural.

But God never wants for us what comes naturally. Instead he wants to make us godly, and sometimes that process takes us into the dark night of the soul.

Christian psychologist Larry Crabb has written about his own struggles with a "darkness in my spirit." "I am starting to regard my struggle with moodiness, at least part of it, as a calling from God rather than a problem to despise or attempt to relieve . . . I sometimes think that the darkness that rushes into my soul like the sudden, dense fog that sweeps across the English countryside is not merely an allergic reaction to chocolate or a product of undisciplined living, but evidence of a gracious God working on my behalf to disengage me from whatever I love more than him."[5]

That's the Nevertheless Principle. The dark despair is there, but God uses it to draw Dr. Crabb—or you and me—closer to him.

"Now I recognize," writes Dr. Crabb, "that low times are part of the maturing process where God is weaning me from every source of joy but Christ, releasing me to enjoy what is good in this life as I wait for the perfect joy ahead."[6]

I don't have darkness sweep over me as Dr. Crabb describes, but I've had times when situations or people have hurt me and driven me to the truth of the Nevertheless Principle. On one occasion several years ago, the leaders of an organization I was deeply involved in made what I felt were false accusations against me. As Jeremiah was wounded under the arrows of his enemy, so I was hurt. I didn't feel I could make a public defense since most people were unaware of what was happening. I also didn't want the organization ripped apart over what was a personal attack. I went before the Lord, asking him to protect my reputation for Christ's sake.

In the middle of this hurtful time, a friend from across the country who knew what was happening sent me a verse:

"You let men ride over our heads;
　　we went through fire and water,
　　but you brought us to a place of abundance." (Ps. 66:12)

Yes! I thought. Men are riding over my head; I am going through fire and water. *Nevertheless,* God will bring me to a place of abundance. Because of this I have hope. I can't get out of the black hole I have fallen in all inadvertently and innocently. But God! Ah, he can and will draw me forth.

And he did.

"Hope is the antithesis of despair," Pastor Rick said. "I have never known a depressive who's done what he/she should—a counselor, a therapist, specific tasks—and who has also trusted God who hasn't gotten better. I'm not saying they will get well and never have to struggle any more. But they will get better."

Apart from Thee,
　　I long and thirst
　　And naught can satisfy.

I wander in a desert land
Where all the streams are dry.
—Hymn 111, *Dutch Reformed Psalter*

QUESTIONS, QUESTIONS

1. Read Isaiah 43:1–3a. Have you been in a place like the writer describes? What is God's promise to you?
2. Read Habakkuk 3:17–19. Why is the word *yet* so important? What does the prophet encourage us to do in distress?
3. Read Psalm 13. What is the mind-set of David in this psalm? What is his answer to his questions?
4. Why is it so hard to trust God? What makes the Nevertheless Principle such a challenge?
5. Read Romans 8:28. What is the qualifier for all things working for good? What does *good* mean?

Chapter 5

An Ungrateful Heart

*I would maintain that thanks are the highest form of thought
and that gratitude is happiness doubled by wonder.*
—G. K. Chesterton

One Christmas when I was about twelve, my brother Chickie,
seven years old, gave me a gift that he had picked out by himself. My
mother had taken him to Woolworth's and left him while she went
about her shopping. Chickie cruised the aisles, looking for just the
right gift for each of us. For days he smiled happily to himself, certain that he had gotten us exactly the presents that would please us
most.

On Christmas morning he handed me the gift he'd selected and
wrapped for me, looking excited and pleased. I, a mature twelve,
opened the little box, curious to see what the kid had come up with.

Nestled in the box I found a small locket shaped as a heart with an open center. It hung on a silver chain.

"Diamonds," Chickie told me proudly, pointing to the cut glass that formed the heart.

"Beautiful," I said unenthusiastically.

He grinned, pleased I liked it. "Now hold it up to the light and look in the center," he said.

I held the gift to the light and looked as told. The center of the heart wasn't open after all. There, before my unbelieving eyes and under a piece of magnifying plastic, was the whole of the Lord's Prayer—if you squinted and used your imagination.

"Isn't it pretty?" Chickie said.

"Great," I said as I looked at my mother in disbelief.

"I knew you liked God and stuff." My brother couldn't have been happier.

I nodded and tried to look appreciative, all the while thinking that there was no way I'd ever be seen in public wearing something so tacky.

"How thoughtful, Chickie," Mom said warmly.

"Yeah," I agreed, smiling at my brother as I reached for my next gift. "Thoughtful."

"Put it on," Chickie said.

I put the ugly thing about my neck, certain I'd have a tarnish ring on my skin when I took it off. As soon as the gifts were all open and Chickie was busy playing with his new toys, I took the locket off, put it in its box, and planned how I could "lose" it.

Later that day Chickie and I went down the street to visit my friend Margie and her brother Frank to see their gifts, a neighborhood kid ritual. Chickie and Frank huddled around Frank's gifts, and Margie and I examined hers.

"So what did you get?" she asked after I'd been properly impressed with her new acquisitions.

I reeled off my list, ending with Chickie's offering. "If you hold it up to the light, you can see the Lord's Prayer!" I looked at Margie to see if she appreciated how awful the heart was. "It's the stupidest—"

Margie grabbed my arm and pointed. Chickie was standing not three feet from me. Suddenly I was struck by how hurt he'd be if he knew what I thought of his carefully selected present. My heart constricted. After all, he was just a little kid, and he'd tried. I didn't want to make him feel bad and ruin his Christmas.

I looked at him carefully. How could I know whether he'd heard? He seemed to be talking with Frank, completely unaware of me. But what if he'd heard and was putting on a brave front? I was willing to apologize, but I knew I couldn't unless I knew he'd heard me. After all, I didn't want to say I was sorry and have him say, "What for?" How could I explain? To this day, I don't know whether he heard my unkind comments or not, and to this day I still feel badly.

This incident is one of my first recollections of my own ungrateful heart. I think it's a powerful one for me because I not only saw myself as a not-very-nice person, but I also recognized the potential hurt that a thankless spirit can inflict.

How many times have any of us carelessly been that ungrateful person?

"Boy, that was a good sermon," someone says.

Someone else shrugs. "If you wanted to take a nap."

Or perhaps you've heard, "Wasn't Margaret thoughtful to do that?"

And the response, "Well, maybe today, but I've seen the other side of her. Not a pretty sight, let me tell you."

And there's always, "I hear you got a new TV."

"Yeah, well, it's too big, the cabinet's ugly, and the color's too intense." Forced laugh. "Other than that, it's fine. What I really wanted was a new washer, but who listens to me?"

Who listens to her indeed. She's done everything to ensure that no one does, but she doesn't realize it. Sad.

Jan came to me to talk because she was alone and hurting and wanted to fix the situation.

"It's probably because my family aren't Christians," she said.

"I don't think that would do it," I said. "Lots of people have family who don't believe."

"But not like mine. My parents keep asking me to leave home and get my own place."

"Well, you're twenty-eight and have a good job as a teacher. Most parents want their children to become self-sufficient and live on their own."

She didn't like that comment, so she ignored it. "They took my bedroom for my mother's office."

"What does your mother do?"

"She's a CPA and has a business from the house."

"So she needs an office."

"No. She's used the dining room table until now, and she can just keep on that way. She doesn't need an office, not when I have to sleep on the living room sofa."

"Have you looked for a possible apartment?"

"I don't want to live alone."

"Have you asked any of the single women you know if they want a roommate?"

"Everybody's getting married. There's no one left."

"No one?"

"No one I'd consider living with."

"Then why not take a one-bedroom place for yourself? It's got to be better than sleeping on the sofa."

"Do you know how expensive that would be?"

I didn't know specifically, but I had an idea. "You make a good salary. There are men and women supporting families on your income. You can make it."

"I have to take graduate classes. All my money goes there."

I knew graduate school was expensive, but I also knew it wasn't that expensive and that there was a good chance she got reimbursed. "What are you taking? I always enjoyed the mental stimulation of classes."

"The professor is so boring. You wouldn't believe! And I have to write three papers and do a major creative project!"

"It is graduate school. It's not supposed to be easy."

"And I have to drive thirty minutes one way. It takes forever!"

"Have you ever thought of listening to books on tape to pass the time on the drive?"

"The library is ten minutes in the opposite direction."

I took a deep breath. I knew that if I told her that the crisp winter day we were enjoying was bright and beautiful, she'd tell me that it had been dark for over twelve hours that very day and what did I think of that?

"Tell me what the Lord has done for you recently," I said, trying to get her off her grumble. Surely if she talked about the Lord, there'd be good things that came to her mind.

She looked at me in silence.

Thinking to encourage her, I said, "If it were me, I'd thank the Lord for my health, the sunshine outside, the Word, our church and pastor, my salvation." I tried not to be Gayle-specific, but to offer her a glimpse of things that she could be legitimately grateful for. As the rain falls on the just and the unjust, so we believers hold many wonderful things in common. Surely she could think of one or two. "What about you?"

Again she just looked at me, and I realized that an ungrateful spirit so gripped her that she literally couldn't think of anything for which to be thankful. My heart broke for her.

She and I met weekly for almost three months, talking about a thankful spirit, the blessings of her life (which were many), and God's commands for us to rejoice and be thankful. We talked about putting off complaining and putting on being grateful in its place. We practiced this spiritual skill. At the end she was no more willing to be grateful than when we started. To this day, when she and I talk, she has nothing that pleases her. She's now in her forties, still single and still living at home, though I don't know if she still has to sleep on the sofa.

Most of us see people like Jan as ridiculous and sad. They see problems where they don't exist, and they expand little things into great issues. Most of us learn the dangers of griping when we are young and try our best to avoid that trap.

Author Robert Fulghum wrote of an older gentleman he met while he himself was still a young man. The older man, Sigmund Wollman, was a Holocaust survivor of Auschwitz. One night when Fulghum was complaining about his boss, Wollman said, "Lissen me. You know what's wrong with you? You don't know the difference between an inconvenience and a problem. If you break your neck, if you have nothing to eat, if your house is on fire—then you got a problem. Everything else is inconvenient. Life is inconvenient. Life is lumpy."[1]

But sometimes, you say, there are real issues and genuine problems in our lives that almost demand a good bout of complaining.

In *Alice in Wonderland,* Alice found a little vial with a note that read, "Drink me." She did and ended up three inches tall.

"'Are you content now?' asked the caterpillar.

"'Well, I should like to be a little taller,' she said. 'Three inches is such a wretched height to be. . . . I'm not used to it.'"

If I were Alice, suddenly three inches tall, I'm sure I'd feel I had a right to feel wretched too—and let everyone know it. Unfortunately for us as Christians, the Word doesn't give us a sliding scale delineating issues terrible enough for griping, mild enough for a cozy grouse, and fine enough to allow nothing but praise. "I've learned *whatever* the circumstances," Paul wrote, "to be content."

An ungrateful heart is as old as mankind. Lot is an early example of one who didn't see the things he had to be thankful for but rather took and took until he put himself and his family in mortal danger.

Lot was orphaned when his father Haran died. We don't know how old Lot would have been at this time, but the Bible notes that Haran died before his own father Terah. In other words, Haran died young, and probably left a young son in Lot. Grandfather Terah took Lot into his home and raised him. When Terah left his home in Ur of the Chaldeans, he took his young grandson Lot with him as well as Abram, his son and Lot's uncle, and Sarai, Abram's wife. The family traveled to the land of Canaan.

When Terah died, Lot remained with Abram, and together they accumulated much wealth. Eventually the two men owned so many herds that there was no longer room for them to remain part of the same camp. Their herdsmen had begun fighting over land and water.

"I don't like the fighting between us," Abram said to his nephew. "After all, we're family. I'm afraid we're going to have to part company. There's all this land before us. If you decide to go right, I'll go left. If you decide to go left, I'll go right. You pick."

Lot nodded, liking what he heard. He was being given first dibs. He looked around and saw that the most fertile, well-watered land was the plain of the Jordan River. It was so rich that it looked like a garden. And he grabbed it. All of it.

What an ungrateful move. Lot had been taken in by Terah and watched over by his Uncle Abram. The associations had not only given him a family when he needed one but also made him a rich man. Now, instead of sharing the bounty of the plain with Abram, which seems the least he could do as a gesture of thanks for all Abram and his family had done for him, Lot seized all the best land for himself. He and his family went to live on the plain, pitching their tents near Sodom. Later the family moved into Sodom.

Abram went up into the mountains of Canaan to Mamre and settled beneath the great trees there, blessed by God because of his great heart.

This sad little story of Lot teaches us three things about ungrateful people.

1. Ungrateful people, never satisfied, grasp for more and more, always thinking that the next thing will make them happy.

Surely more herds will do it. That's not enough? Well, then the whole plain's the secret. No? Then it must be living in the sophisticated city of Sodom.

Frequently, as with Lot, in the end the things selfishly grasped sting like a nettle. That is the price for having an ungrateful spirit. Oh, we won't find ourselves, as Lot did, captured by an enemy king and ignominiously rescued by Uncle Abraham. We won't end up fleeing a city being destroyed by heaven-sent fire and brimstone or losing our spouses when disobedience makes them pillars of salt. We won't commit incest with our daughters while drunk.

But our ungratefulness can easily lead to our taking advantage of people. It can cause us to value things above people and, more dangerously, above God.

2. Ungrateful people run roughshod over the people in their lives.

Time and again Lot took advantage of Abram's kindness. My friend Jan took advantage of her parents' home, all the while complaining about them. I was careless of my little brother's feelings.

Pain and hurt follow an ungrateful person much like a billowing train trails the bride. Unfortunately only the latter is beautiful.

3. An ungrateful heart leads us farther and farther from truly knowing God.

First we're dissatisfied with life. That emotion turns into dissatisfaction with God's choices for us, which eventually becomes dissatisfaction with God himself. After all, if he really loved us, would he allow us to be so unhappy, so deprived, so hard pressed?

I've learned a fourth thing about the ungrateful by listening to folks like Jan talk.

4. An ungrateful person blames her unhappiness on others.

It's my mother's fault I have to sleep on the sofa. It's my friends' fault that I can't find a roommate I like because they're all getting married. It's the professor's fault that class is hard. It's the college's fault that the drive is long.

The truth of the matter is that an ungrateful heart comes naturally to all of us. Some of us have a greater predilection to complain than others, just as some of us are more easily despairing, more easily angered, more easily proud. But at times all of us are ungrateful, if only by default. We simply don't appreciate what we have materially and spiritually.

I think this casual attitude toward our blessings is very American. Most of us have never been without, so we don't appreciate what we have. We don't notice our bounty. We have become *uh-sure women.*

Uh-sure women take things for granted. They expect a nice house, a cordless phone, a closet full of clothes. They expect regular paychecks and going out for dinner a couple of times a week. It's like these things are givens in life, and if they're missing, uh-sure women feel shortchanged. But if these things are present, they are unappreciated. It's what life's supposed to be like.

"You got another new car, Kay?"

"Uh, sure. We get one every couple of years."

"Marion, I hear you got a new kitchen."

"Uh, sure. I was tired of the old cabinets."

Uh-sure women not only take things for granted, but worse yet, they take people for granted.

"Wasn't it wonderful of Mom to cook that special dinner for the whole family, all seventeen of us?"

"Uh, sure. Wonderful." Moms are supposed to cook for the family. Families are supposed to get together. Big deal.

"Your husband gave you that gorgeous ring for your birthday?"

"Uh, sure." Husbands are supposed to give gifts, big gifts, on birthdays. After all, I'm worth it.

Worst of all, uh-sure women take God for granted. They don't actively rant and rail against him, but they never think to praise or thank him either. Good health? Uh, sure. That's the way it's supposed to be. Beautiful weather? Uh, sure. That's God's job. A good income? Uh, sure. That's to be expected.

If we're uh-sure women, it's all about us.

"But it isn't about us," novelist and editor Karen Ball says. "It isn't about what makes us happy or makes us feel good. It's about him and how well we reflect him to the world around us. It's surrendering 'my rights.' I'm not my own; I was bought with a terrifying price. And the blood that saved me marks me as one who must lay down my so-called rights, looking to the Master to see what he asks of me, not what I think I deserve. My job is to obey as willingly and lovingly as I can, with a heart of gratitude for my life."

It is a given that all of us have things in our lives that we dislike. Living in a sinful world, how could it be different? The big issue revolves around how we deal with these things. Too many of us go the uh-sure woman one step farther and become *bah-humbug women.*

All of us know the story of Charles Dickens's *A Christmas Carol.* We know how Scrooge has a bah-humbug attitude toward life in general and Christmas in particular. He is the epitome of the ungrateful heart, a man with money and position who complains about everything, uses his power to abuse, and sneers at Christian charity. He has no grace, no appreciation for the good things his life could hold.

It's easy to shake our heads in disbelief at Mr. Scrooge because his attitude is so blatant. He, like the teenager who snarls at her family and then shuts herself in her room with her own TV, computer, CD player, and private phone line, is an ungrateful, bah-humbug person. We recognize the wrong attitude immediately, especially if we happen to live with someone like him.

But what about me? Do I recognize a bah-humbug attitude in myself when it's present? Do I grouse and complain even as I take advantage of the services or kindnesses offered me? Do too many of my sentences begin, "Yeah, but . . ."? Am I telling stories about my husband (or kids or boss or pastor) that continually put them in a bad light? Do I look for the failures of people before I look for their achievements?

Am I Lot? Or perhaps Jan?

An Ungrateful Heart

The gift of grumbling is largely dispensed among those who have no other talents, or who keep what they have wrapped in a napkin.

—Charles Haddon Spurgeon

Ouch. That hurts.

I don't know about you, but I don't want to be an uh-sure woman or a bah-humbug woman. I don't want to be satisfied with doing what comes naturally. I want to learn to be godly, to be an *ah-yes! woman.* I want to be one who appreciates what God has done for her and who thanks people for their care on her behalf. I want to be the woman who looks at the bad things in her life, not denying them, but learning to see the benefits derived from them, learning to be content in them.

"I firmly believe in the 'lot' theory of life," writes novelist James Scott Bell. "We are all given our 'lot' by God. That is our portion, for which we should be grateful. And gratitude is the key to happiness. I'm so grateful for what I've been given that I don't want to spoil it by self-absorption. Sometimes I really have to work at it, but that's good. It teaches me to trust him all the more."

As part of my "lot" in life, I have suffered from upper back pain for almost thirty years now. Sometimes it's so debilitating it sends me to bed. Other times it just causes low-grade headaches and discomfort. Many times I have complained about my condition to the Lord, asking for healing, telling him I know he can do it, as if I could somehow jolly him into doing what I want.

He has shown me through the years that if I want to be an ah-yes! woman, a woman of a grateful spirit, then I have to look at this negative thing and search for positive meanings or blessings. I have to put off the old way of thinking—that chronic pain is terrible—

and renew my mind. A new thought pattern would be that God can use terrible things like pain in a positive manner if we are willing.

"All right, Father. Instead of being ungrateful and angry that this pain has lasted all these years, I want to look for the good things you can teach me through this pain. I want to be grateful even in this."

God has taught me three things about my pain:

1. I have learned to be more understanding of others in pain or difficulty. Since I'm a doer and an achiever, I had very little understanding of limitations except in the broadest of senses. I now have at least some idea of what others might be suffering in a chronic situation.

2. Through the pain I have been forced to depend on God and on others, two things that are difficult for me. I like to call the shots, to be the one in command. My need has forced me to be dependent. How good this has been for me.

3. My pride has also taken a needed blow. Not only do I have a limitation; I have one that doesn't even show. I have to *tell* others that I can't carry in the groceries today or I can't hold the crying baby or I can't sit in that chair with the puffy back. I have to admit to being weak—because I am.

On a sillier but still vital note, we live in a small house, a three-bedroom ranch. It's a nice house, don't get me wrong, but we originally thought of it as our starter home. Instead we've been in it for almost thirty years. Most of our friends have larger homes. Our kids have larger homes. I could easily have become a bah-humbug individual over this house, but I chose to put on the new way of looking at it. Two benefits from living in this smaller home are:

1. I have less housework to do. For me this is a big thing. I don't enjoy cleaning. I like to fix the place up, play interior designer, but then I'd like it to stay clean and neatly arranged forever. Fat chance

of that ever happening. A smaller place with less to clean and straighten gives me more time to write, to spend with my family, to do other things of interest to me.

2. Our finances aren't tied in such a tight knot that we have no discretionary monies. Because of a smaller house and smaller mortgage payments, we have more money to give to the Lord, the funds to take trips with our kids and build memories, and the ability to help others in need.

We vacation annually at a lake in Canada, and one of the grandest things about the place is the stars at night. We go down to the dock and look up into a sky not dimmed by city lights. The Milky Way is directly overhead, a blanket of soft white against the black sky. The Big Dipper dumps its unseen load while the Little Dipper ladles its treasure. Pleiades clusters just to the right, and Orion's belt lies crisp and straight behind us. On occasion we have watched a rain of falling stars, brilliant trails tracing the sky for but an instant.

We're like these gleaming testimonies to a Creator, says Paul, as we "do everything without complaining or arguing, so that you may become blameless and pure, children of God without fault in a crooked and depraved generation, in which you shine like stars in the universe as you hold out the word of life" (Phil. 2:14–16a).

Somehow I like the idea of our being stars for Jesus, pulsing, living flames that testify to the remarkable new creation God has made us and is continuing to make us.

Instead of:

> Star light, star bright,
> First star I see tonight,
> I wish I may, I wish I might
> Have the wish I wish tonight.

We can say:

> Star light, star bright,
> Sisters in our Lord, tonight
> Let us shine with all his might
> To turn the world to Christ tonight.

QUESTIONS, QUESTIONS

1. Write five general blessings God has given you. Write five spiritual blessings God has given you. Write five specific, personal-only-to-you blessings God has given you.

2. List three areas in which you could develop an ungrateful heart. Write two positive things that can come from these potentially negative areas.

3. Read 2 Corinthians 12:9–10. How do these verses apply to developing a grateful heart?

4. Read Psalm 107:1, 8–9. What things is the psalmist thankful for? How many of these things apply to you?

5. Read 1 Thessalonians 5:16–18. What does it mean to give thanks in all circumstances?

Chapter 6

Regret

If the problem-side of the scale seems heavy,
then focus on the glory-side. When you do,
you're a Rumpelstilskin weaving straw into gold.
—Joni Eareckson Tada and Steven Estes, *When God Weeps*

The note slid under my door and skittered across the floor of my room at the retreat center where I was the weekend speaker. I picked it up and opened it.

About seven years ago I was involved with a guy in college. I got pregnant. I was so scared and confused. I agreed to have an abortion. I have never regretted any decision as much as that one.

Intellectually I know that God can and will forgive any sin, even one as terrible as this one. But I can't forgive myself. I don't feel I deserve to be forgiven. That somehow that would be disloyal to my child.

Please, give some hope and guidance on how to forgive myself.
There was no signature.

I went to the door and peered down the hall, but whoever had written the note was nowhere in sight. I wasn't surprised. If there was no signature, obviously the woman wanted anonymity. But how could I answer her questions if I didn't know who she was? And what was the answer anyway?

I sat down and thought. My first reaction was, *Lord, give me a break! How can I ever deal with a sensitive topic like this—and on the spur of the moment?* My second thought was, *How can I not?*

My problem was that I had no study materials or books with me. All I had were my teaching notes for the weekend and my "teaching Bible," a worn leather volume that was well broken in and easy to handle but hadn't even the simplest of concordances in it.

"Help, Lord!"

It wasn't understanding the woman's difficulty that bothered me. Not at all. In fact, I had an immediate spark of recognition. While I've never had an abortion, I've experienced the same feelings as she, only over different issues, and all prompted by one thing: GUILT laced with regret.

"Help, Lord!" I called again, and we went to work, the Holy Spirit and I.

"I know God has forgiven me, but I can't forgive myself," my unknown woman wrote. Certainly anyone burdened with such guilt doesn't feel contented. To that woman the peace that God planned for us as believers is like the bubble that a child blows from a sudsy wand. It shimmers with iridescent promise and delicate beauty, but it is untouchable, unattainable, fragile, and beyond grasping.

How do we get from guilt ridden and full of regret to contented, resting peacefully in the Lord? Is such a journey even possible? Let's see.

Forgiving ourselves has become an accepted, pop-psychology concept. We hear it on TV and read about it in books and magazines. There's a whole mini-industry of seminars that addresses this very issue.

"You can't be happy until you forgive yourself."

"Only when you forgive yourself can you unlock your true potential."

We're even instructed on the topic from pulpits: "Forgive yourself. God can't do much with you until you have forgiven yourself and are a clean vessel for him to use."

The phrase is so pervasive and the concept so accepted that you never know when you'll run into it. Several years ago at a Christian writer's conference, I related a story of some shenanigans that got me in trouble one Sunday when as a teenager I worked at a very strict Bible conference.

"I even stripped the tape off the coin slot on the soda machine which was very much off-limits on the Lord's day," I shared. "I've rarely heard a louder noise than those sodas falling. I felt like I'd committed the ultimate in depravity."

Everyone who heard the story laughed except the woman across the table who looked at me very seriously. "It's obvious," she said, "that you've never forgiven yourself."

I blinked at her as did most of the others at the table. Forgiven myself? For what? For peeling Scotch tape off the coin slot? For getting sodas on a Sunday? Surely she wasn't serious. One look at her face showed that she was.

I was appalled that someone who had never before met me would make such a judgment about me, especially based on such a light-hearted story. I was also struck anew by the pervasiveness of the "forgive yourself" mentality.

Perhaps it's time to rethink this whole concept of guilt and regret and forgiving ourselves. It's time to evaluate it in the light of Scripture.

Certainly the most magnificent revelation of Scripture apart from the character of God himself is the story of redemption and forgiveness. It's the scarlet cord that threads its way through the glorious and scandalous tapestry of history. Man's fallen nature, thoughtfully and thoroughly documented by scholars through the ages, needed something drastic to restore it to God, and Christ's sacrificial death is that extravagant, love-drenched, agony-filled solution.

God has never shirked from the reality of our sin. The Word states very clearly that all of us have sinned and fallen short of the glory of God (Rom. 3:23). Nor has God ever denied the harm sin does to us and those we know and love, breaking relationships, ruining friendships, and fracturing families. Scripture shows very openly the trauma sin caused in the lives of biblical characters.

The miracle is that instead of holding us accountable for our actions, our gracious God sent his Son to die in our stead. If we believe in Jesus as our Savior, God then sends our sin away. He declares us not guilty. Judicially we are exonerated. He chooses to treat us not as we deserve but as beloved ones.

"Thou hast treated me," wrote Madame Guyon, a seventeenth-century mystic, "as a king who marries a poor slave, forgets her slavery, gives her what she needs to be beautiful, and pardons her faults and selfish qualities. My poverty has become my riches, and in my extreme weakness I have found strength."[1]

"This is what God does when He forgives: he breaks down the walls we build and gets into the backyard of our souls to make a new relationship."[2]

The backyard of our souls. I love that phrase. It conjures up a picture of home and safety and that which is highly individual. The walls we built for so many years to protect our true selves from God's eyes are gone. Instead, in that most private part of our being, our Father God is building something new in us.

When our guys were little, they had a metal sandbox in the backyard. When it finally rusted through, we got rid of it. We were left with a patch of dirt where the grass had been killed for lack of sun. Before Chuck could get around to seeding the spot, the boys discovered the joy of digging in dirt. Over the years the dirt hole grew wider as it deepened. Towns, construction sites, winding roads, hideouts, all containing countless Matchbox cars and trucks, blossomed as little minds imagined great things.

When God moves into our soul's backyard, it's sort of like the boys moving into that dirt hole. He digs and moves soil, breaks up dirt clods, and realigns our previous boundaries. In the peace and security of our spiritual backyard, he develops new character in us, new dreams, new ventures. The gentle trowel of our Father God makes us deeper, broadens our hearts, and fills us with limitless possibilities.

"When you were dead in your sins and in the uncircumcision of your sinful nature, God made you alive with Christ. He forgave us all our sins" (Col. 2:13).

As we read in the Word about the grace-bathed forgiveness extended to us by God, we also read about our responsibility to forgive one another, not because people always deserve our forgiveness but because we are instructed to offer it. Just as God doesn't deny we've sinned, so we don't deny the wrongs done to us. Nor do we brood on them or suppress them. We acknowledge them in all their ugliness and pain. Then, because of Christ and by choice, we send these hurts, these offenses away. We choose not to recall them. We yield our rights to redress; we give up our plans to get even. We abandon our hopes to receive an apology and our expectations of being understood. We forgive, and we do it out of obedience, just as God in Christ has forgiven us.

"Bear with each other and forgive whatever grievances you may have against one another. Forgive as the Lord forgave you" (Col. 3:13).

So God forgives us in Christ, and we are instructed to forgive one another, but where in the Bible does it talk about forgiving ourselves? At the retreat that fall afternoon in my room with the Murphy bed and poor lighting, I wracked my memory.

"Lord, call to my mind any verses that apply," I begged. All those years of Scripture memory to earn weeks at camp were finally going to pay off. I sat back and waited for the miracle of recall.

However nothing percolated to the top. The more I thought and prayed, the more I came to realize that *nowhere in Scripture do we find instruction to forgive ourselves.*

"Wait a minute! It must be there somewhere! Otherwise why would everyone be talking about it?"

While I'm still not certain why so many people are talking about this topic, I am certain of another thing: if it were important, God would have told us about it in his Word. We know that Scripture contains everything we need for faith and practice. Silence on this subject must mean that for some reason God doesn't see forgiving ourselves as vital.

Then why do people see this issue as so important? Perhaps it's that we humans like to be in on anything of significance, and certainly eternal and daily forgiveness are issues of great magnitude.

But I think that's a secondary reason if it's a valid reason at all. I'd say the main reason forgiving ourselves is such a hot issue is that we frequently live with deep regrets over our past actions. Certainly my note writer fits into this category. "I have never regretted anything as much."

Regret

The word *regret* comes from the Old French *regreter,* which meant to bewail the dead. *Regret* means to feel sorry about, to mourn for, to feel troubled or remorseful over, to sorrow over a person or a thing. We regret anything that diminishes the quality of our lives.

Sometimes we find ourselves regretting something that's not earthshaking but merely deeply embarrassing. It could be an action or something we've said.

The first time Chuck came to our house for dinner when we were dating, it made for an interesting evening. My father is Chuck, my brother is Chuck (his little kid nickname of Chickie had long since gone), and I was throwing another Chuck into the pot.

Part way through dinner, my father decided to pass the potatoes for seconds. "Here, Bob," he said as he handed the dish to my Chuck. "Have some more potatoes."

There was this frozen moment as we all realized Dad had called Chuck by my former boyfriend's name. Then Dad gave a weak little laugh. "I just figured we had too many Chucks around here already."

My Chuck laughed, held out his hand, and took the potatoes. Dinner—and the rest of the evening—progressed uneventfully.

Not long after Chuck left, my father was at the door of my room. He looked worried.

"Do you think I upset him when I called him Bob? I didn't mean that crack about too many Chucks the way it sounded. I certainly don't want to scare him away. After all, he's the best thing you've brought home yet."

There are also regrets over things that never actually happened but could have. When we think of potential consequences because of what we did or didn't do, we turn cold all over.

When I was in seventh grade, it was a new and very adult thing to be able to go to the local football games with my friends, something that was quite safe back then in our small town. One Saturday as I was going out the front door to meet my friends, I heard my mother calling me. Convinced she had another chore for me to do, I kept on going.

Later I learned that she had walked out onto the back porch where the floor gave way under her, plunging her right leg through the wood into the space beneath. Dad wasn't home, so I was her best available help, and she was calling out of very real need. Even today I cringe when I think about what could have happened if a sharp piece of wood or a nail had pierced her skin or worse yet, her femoral artery. I regret I didn't respond as I should have.

Sometimes we regret things that happen through no intent or malice on our part. These things are true accidents, often tragic.

Several years ago I read in the newspaper about a grandfather who was walking into the kitchen carrying at his side the sharp knife they had used outside for a family cookout. Someone said something behind him and he turned to respond, arcing the knife as he did. Unbeknownst to him, his three-year-old granddaughter had danced up to his side. When he turned with the knife in his hand, he caught her with the blade and killed her.

And then there are the things we do that are wrong and we know it. We might have yielded to them because of a rebellious spirit or anger at God or societal pressure like our note writer. Whatever the reason, we knowingly do something we come to regret immensely at a later time. Our stomachs cramp, our palms sweat, and our mouths go dry when we think of these things. Perhaps it's a cruel, malicious comment. Perhaps it's a theft that seemed such a lark at the time. Perhaps it's an abortion. Who knows? Our consciences just can't deal well with whatever our memories hold.

One thing is certain about our memories and the past: they are unchangeable. No matter how much we wish for time to roll back until just before we made our mistake, it won't happen. Maybe time travel is so appealing to science fiction and fantasy writers and readers because it allows the characters to change circumstances in a way real life never does. If a character can go back in time and prevent two characters from meeting, thus preventing a tragedy in the future, writers and readers feel a sense of control denied them in real life.

The apostle Paul certainly had many things to regret about his past. He had persecuted the church with great zeal, killing and jailing believers. Now suddenly with his conversion he was on the other side of things, one of the persecuted. But how could he forget the pain he'd caused? How could he deal with the distress of having killed innocent men and women? Having orphaned children?

"Brothers, I do not consider myself yet to have taken hold of it," he writes. "But one thing I do: Forgetting what is behind and straining toward what is ahead, I press on toward the goal to win the prize for which God has called me heavenward in Christ Jesus" (Phil. 3:13–14).

Forget what's behind is Paul's first step in dealing with regrets. Since the past is immutable, then we should just forget it.

When we are encouraged to forget what's behind, it's with the idea of setting our minds on something else. Obviously we have to think about something. It's impossible to have an empty mind. So instead of thinking of the past and all the regrets, we fill our thoughts with the future, or as Paul said, we *strain* toward what's ahead.

When I was a kid, we had an amiable boxer named Clipper. Kindly put, Clipper was no threat whatsoever to Lassie and Rin Tin Tin intellectually. To try to help cure his abominable, if friendly, manners, Mom decided to take Clipper to obedience school. The dog loved school. A gregarious sort, he had a wonderful time nosing around all the other dogs, leaning against all their owners, and in general driving his trainer crazy. Twice Mom took him through the program, and twice Clipper happily failed.

He did learn one thing though. Whenever Mom put on a certain plaid shirt, it was time to go to class and have fun. He'd strain into his leash, eager to get going. He'd pull Mom to the car and sit in the front seat, panting in excitement. At class the thought of sitting or heeling was far from his mind. He was too busy straining forward, his button of a tail wagging in delight at the thought of being with all his wonderful new friends.

That's a good picture of how we should be as we strain ahead, though hopefully we'll move forward with a bit more savvy and wisdom than Clipper. Our Father has something wonderful waiting for each of us around the nearest corner, and it's much more exciting by far than what we're leaving behind.

First we forget what's behind, then we strain ahead, and lastly we *press* on toward our goal of serving the Lord somehow. Think of a runner pressing forward, leaning toward the tape as he goes for the win. He doesn't look back to see what's behind him. It has become immaterial. It is only what's ahead that matters, and it matters the entire length of the race.

"OK," you say. "So we shouldn't get swamped with regrets. So the Bible doesn't talk about forgiving myself. So it says I should forget the past. Well, you don't know what I did!"

That's the way the young woman who wrote me that note felt when she referred to her abortion as "even (an action) as terrible as this one."

It's common when we are plagued by guilt to think of our actions as the ultimate in sin. Even if intellectually we know there are things that seem worse or people who routinely do worse, because of our sore heart, we know what we've done is beyond forgiving. We don't deserve to be free of it. Isn't that what my note writer said? "I don't deserve to be forgiven."

And of course we don't. None of us do. We are, after all, guilty. But the choice to offer forgiveness is God's, not ours. He looked down at us, saw what a sorry mess we were making of our lives, and declared himself willing to put aside our sins in Christ's name and for the sake of his love. When he made this choice, he didn't rate our sins as to awfulness.

What we've forgotten or perhaps never known is that *all sin is an offense to God's holiness.* It's not a case of "Uh-oh, look at her. She needs more forgiveness. And her! Wow, will she be a challenge to forgive!"

No, not at all. Sin is sin in his eyes, all hurtful and offensive to a perfect God.

> There are six things the LORD hates,
>   seven that are detestable to him:
> haughty eyes,
> a lying tongue,
> hands that shed innocent blood,
> a heart that devises wicked schemes,
> feet that are quick to rush into evil,
> a false witness who pours out lies
> and a man who stirs up dissension among brothers.
>   (Prov. 6:16–19)

That's a very interesting collection of offenses. In our human eyes some certainly seem worse than others. But Solomon reminds us that they are all hated by God.

Who of us hasn't had a few proud moments or told a lie or two or two hundred?

"Yes," the guilt-filled person wants to shout, "but that's not as bad as what I did! You just don't know what I did!"

Remember, all these sins are lumped together as things that are detestable to God. Saying something that's not really true about someone is as wrong in God's eyes as the shedding of the innocent blood of an unborn child or a living adult, as wrong as feeling prideful or stirring up feelings against a pastor.

Certainly some wrongs have greater consequences than others. There can be no debate on that truth. I imagine that we excuse some sins and assign additional blame to others because of the results we see. But God runs, as it were, an equal opportunity shop. Therefore the thing we have done that is eating us alive is no more sinful than the sin we readily forgive in others.

Still we struggle with the all-sins-are-equally-offensive logic because Satan, the great accuser (Rev. 12:10), knows our vulnerability and goes after us. If he can accuse us again and again of the same wrong, he can drive a wedge between us and our Father. Instead of approaching the throne of mercy with confidence, we find ourselves coming hesitantly, apologetically. We act as if our Father is angry with us or disappointed in us when he is really accepting and forgiving, longing for our company.

"Let us draw near to God with a sincere heart in full assurance of faith, having our hearts sprinkled to cleanse us from a guilty conscience and having our bodies washed with pure water" (Heb. 10:22).

A third thing strikes me when we worry about forgiving ourselves. I believe it shows a flawed view of the cost of our forgiveness. *We demonstrate a view of God's forgiveness that is too low and a view of ourselves that is too high.*

When Christ died on the cross, he washed us of all our sins. All. Every single one—ones we deem big and ones we think too small to even mention. When we believed, he forgave us entirely. Absolutely. "If we confess our sins, he is faithful and just and will forgive us our sins and purify us from *all* unrighteousness" (1 John 1:9, italics mine).

The blood of Christ isn't like bleach, which makes the stain seem to disappear when in reality it still exists, visible in certain kinds of light. Jesus' cleansing is total, his forgiveness absolute.

If we insist on forgiving ourselves, we are saying—intentionally or not—that the atonement wasn't sufficient. The sin stain still lingers, visible to our perceptive eye, and only we can deal with it. We are telling God, "I'm sorry. It's not that I don't appreciate what Jesus did for me. I really do, and I mean no offense. But I have to forgive myself, or this issue in my life isn't properly handled."

If we think carefully about such a mind-set, we will be struck by our egotism. *Jesus can't do it all. He needs my help.*

I have a memory with which I struggled for a long time. Regret mingled with guilt, and any time the memory came to mind, I was spiritually paralyzed, even though I had not fallen into that particular sin in many years, even though I'd confessed it way back when. I felt like David when he cried, "My guilt has overwhelmed me like a burden too heavy to bear" (Ps. 38:4).

"Oh, God, I'm so sorry!" I'd cry time after time.

Then in one of those wonderful moments of God-granted insight, I realized I had no need to ask forgiveness for that particular sin. It had been forgiven years ago, the first time I'd confessed. Every time I cried anew for release from guilt, I was denying the effectiveness of Christ's death. I was saying he gave his life for the sins of the whole world, and all who believe had received his absolution—except me. I was still in trouble over this particular issue.

How utterly presumptuous! How dare I demean forgiveness bought at so great and terrifying a price!

This insight was the first step in claiming what was already mine as a child of God. I got down on my knees beside my bed and acknowledged that Christ had forgiven all my sins, even the one that haunted me. Then I confessed that my constant feelings of guilt came from myself, not from him. I repeated 1 John 1:9 aloud as the proof of my new thinking.

I knelt and made a small ceremony because I wanted to remember the moment. I wanted to have a specific reference point for when the doubts and guilt and regret returned. I knew such a drastic change in thinking wouldn't be automatic. It would take spiritual discipline to believe God instead of my falsely guilty conscience. It would take practice, practice, practice. "The mature . . . by constant use have trained themselves to distinguish good from evil" (Heb. 5:14).

When guilt returned, I refused it. I quoted 1 John 1:9, often out loud for the extra oomph of hearing the words as well as thinking them. When I first began this process, I found I had to repeat the promise of Scripture frequently. Old thought patterns die hard.

I have a friend with her own issues. She pictures herself putting her burden in God's arms and walking out of the room.

"Some days I have to do that a million times, other days not at all," she said. "But Christ is our great Burden Bearer, and I gladly give my burdens to him."

I've also read of the idea of writing on a piece of paper whatever is eating at you. Then burn the paper in a guilt offering, letting go of that sin and accepting the completeness of Christ's atonement. Here again you have a point of reference when the doubts come.

As time passes and we practice the discipline of accepting the forgiveness God has given us, the false guilt will strike less and less. What freedom we will find when we accept God's forgiveness as sufficient, when we truly embrace what we say we believe.

Regret

I shared many of these thoughts on guilt and regret with the women at the retreat, hoping to touch the heart of the woman who had written me the anonymous note. I scanned the crowd of well over a hundred, wondering to whom I was speaking.

On Sunday afternoon, when everyone was saying good-bye, a young woman shook my hand.

"Thank you for coming," she said. Then she leaned in and hugged me. "And thank you," she whispered in my ear, "for giving me hope."

QUESTIONS, QUESTIONS

1. Look again at the things you regret. Have they tied you to the past? How does 1 Peter 5:7 apply?

2. Read 2 Corinthians 7:10. What is the result of godly sorrow? What effect does this verse have on you?

3. Articulate how the put off/put on principle of Ephesians 4:22–24 works in regard to regret and false guilt (guilt you hold on to after God has forgiven you).

4. Read Romans 8:1–2. How does this great promise offer us hope for today and the future?

5. What is the main thing that keeps you from believing 1 John 1:9 actually applies to you?

Chapter 7

Envy

Character is what a man is in the dark.
—D. L. Moody

We were leaving Anna's house after a wonderful evening of food and good company. As we walked up the drive to our cars, Jane said, "Well, I'll be spending the next week asking God to forgive me for envy."

"I know what you mean," said Ashleigh. "Look at this place! If Anna weren't such a nice person, I'd really hate her."

We all laughed because we knew exactly what Jane and Ashleigh meant. Anna's house was right out of *House Beautiful* or *Architectural Digest*. The large wooded lot was carefully landscaped, and the flowers and shrubs were gorgeous. A bench here and a garden statue there gave a warm and individual look to the yard. Even the neighbor's marmalade cat sleeping beside an azalea looked too good to be true.

And inside everything was equally perfect. Not only did Anna have wonderful taste herself; she had the pocketbook to hire a professional interior decorator and to purchase the items recommended. Add to that family china and silver, linen table settings, original art, unique decorator pieces from Anna's travels, and bright masses of flowers. The house was a feast for the eyes and senses, enough to make anyone envious.

I have to tell you, though, that I didn't want Anna's house. I kept thinking of all the work it would take to keep it so beautiful. No, if I were to envy Anna, it would be for her long legs.

Only those of you whose feet never quite touch the ground when seated will understand the feelings of a short-legged person. I have to hem even petite slacks. There's something very sad about the fact that the only place I can count on putting my feet flat on the floor is in an automobile with its low-slung seats.

I hear all you long-legged women moaning that I haven't the vaguest idea of the difficulties of trying to find slacks long enough or airline seats with enough leg room between them. I imagine those issues give difficulty, but never forget that all the models have long legs. And they and you look good in all sorts of clothes! We short-legged wonders can look sawed off at the knees if we're not very careful.

I'm sure some women would envy Anna her husband, a sweet guy with a wonderful job who clearly dotes on her and their kids. And other women would want her wardrobe or maybe her warm personable nature or her organizational abilities or her Jacuzzi tub or . . .

My point is that there is always more than enough around us to envy. It takes no great thought and less talent to do so. Envy just comes naturally, like breathing or scratching an itch. In fact, envy is one way of scratching the itch of not having what we'd like or not being what we wish.

Perhaps one of the most fascinating things about envy is that we frequently envy that which we are powerless to change, like my short legs.

Joyce, an insurance underwriter for a large company, coveted Patti's boss, of all things. Joyce's own boss was grumpy and very demanding, and he didn't hesitate to yell if displeased—which he frequently was. Patti's boss was a kind man with an upbeat disposition who got everyone under him to produce by praising them. When Patti, a medical technician in a large lab, talked about her boss, Joyce felt a slow burn.

"Next thing I know, you're going to tell me he walks on water," she snipped.

Patti blinked but said nothing, though she wondered why the venom.

Later when Joyce complained about her boss and Patti sympathized, Joyce resented the sympathy. "You can't possibly understand what I'm talking about," she said nastily. "You work for Mr. Perfect."

Since Patti liked her boss, she took Joyce's unwarranted attacks personally. She stopped talking about him around Joyce, which was hard since she loved to talk about her work. Of course, Joyce complained about her own boss incessantly.

"Don't blame me for your boss," Patti said after one evening full of complaints and barbed comments. "It's not my fault he's mean."

"Oh, I suppose you think it's mine?"

"What?"

"Nothing," was Joyce's classic answer, and a long-standing friendship was damaged and slowly died.

Over a boss!

Over a boss that Joyce couldn't work under no matter how much she wanted to because they were in different industries!

So what do we do when we can't change a situation? Take my legs for an example. I can't change their length. But I have learned to appreciate them in spite of the fact that I take two steps to my husband's one, and he always wonders why I tire more quickly than he when we walk.

When I think about it, short legs always let me be near the front of the line in the old days back at school. Short legs always get me in the front for a group picture, thus saving me from being the part of a head barely visible behind Uncle Joe. Short legs get me up front along a parade route, assuring me of missing nothing. And short legs are, after all, what God gave me.

The spiritually scary thing about envy is that even when we know we can't change the circumstances that are leading us to envy, if we don't put off envy and put on acceptance and appreciation, we will fall more deeply into envy's cold embrace.

We will think things that not only turn us from God but make us wretched. We will say things that not only hurt people but cost us friends. We might even do things that are out-and-out nasty or harmful. And all because we compared what we had with what we wanted or wanted to be.

"Comparison fuels the fire of envy within people. It prompts the tendency to judge . . . it makes us prejudiced people."[1]

"I think one's level of contentment has everything to do with whom you compare yourself to," says novelist Deborah Raney. "I can stand in my front yard and look north to our little town's gorgeous golf course and the half-million-dollar homes that line its fairways and think, *Lord, why couldn't I be so blessed? Why can't I live in such luxury?* or I can turn my head and look south to the town's trailer park and think, *Lord, I am so blessed. I live in such luxury! Thank you, Father!* My circumstances haven't changed one iota, but my perspective makes all the difference in the world. I try really hard to keep my perspective southward."

"On the comparison issue," writes children's author Sandra Byrd. "I constantly remind myself not to look to the right nor to the left at others. If I'm looking at Sally on the left or Bob on the right, I've taken my eyes off of looking up—for direction—and forward—where I need to step next. It's almost a mantra to me when I'm tempted to compare—'neither to the left nor to the right.'"

Let's consider Suzie who constantly compares herself to Anna of the beautiful house. On one hand, Suzie resents Anna because she has what Suzie wants—a good education, a lovely home, a loving husband, good kids, and lots of friends. The last one is the issue that irks Suzie most since she has few friends herself. She knows that if she had friends like Anna, she would find a husband like Anna's, and then everything else would follow. Sometimes, on bad days, Suzie is even willing to contemplate taking Terry away from Anna.

While on the one hand Suzie resents Anna, on the other she wants to be just like Anna. She wants to look like Anna in spite of the fact that Anna has dark hair and eyes and Suzie is fair with hazel eyes. Suzie wants to get along with people like Anna does in spite of the fact that Anna is a marvelous listener and Suzie is a compulsive talker. Suzie wants to be respected for her spiritual insights like Anna is in spite of the fact that her spiritual gift, when she bothers to use it, is helping.

Suzie spends a lot of time thinking about Anna, letting her envy grow deep, becoming a root of bitterness that is sending up poisonous shoots to taint her whole life.

Look at her, Suzie thinks as she watches people talk to Anna after the Sunday service. *Playing to the crowd. She's so sweet it gives me cavities just watching.*

At the same time she eyes Anna's new suit, knowing that if she could afford something that nice, she'd look pretty too. *Maybe one of the outlets,* she thinks, not realizing that the vivid red that looks wonderful on dark Anna will eat her fairness alive. When she does find a similar outfit and buys it, she resents Anna even more because it doesn't look on her as it did on Anna. And people don't compliment her as they did Anna.

And the dark thoughts get darker. The root of bitterness winds ever more tightly about her heart, and the next thing Suzie knows, she's voicing these critical and demeaning thoughts.

"Did you see Anna on Sunday?" she asks a friend on the phone in that have-I-got-news-for-you tone of voice. "I don't know how Terry puts up with it."

"What are you talking about? She was just the same as always."

"You think so? Well, I won't say any more."

And finally a day may come when Suzie begins to flirt with Terry or tell outright lies about Anna. And it all started in the mind with envy.

We like to believe that what's in our mind isn't harmful because it's private. No one else is being influenced or harmed by our imaginings, especially because most thoughts remain no more than thoughts. If we acted out what we were pondering, then we would be wrong.

Not so. Jesus told the crowd that lusting in the imagination was as bad as adultery. That particular teaching raised the bar of mental purity very high. The truth is: as we think, so are we.

"Finally, brothers, whatever is true, whatever is noble, whatever is right, whatever is pure, whatever is lovely, whatever is admirable—if anything is excellent or praiseworthy—think about such things" (Phil. 4:8).

It's easy to think like Suzie. As we noted earlier, it comes naturally. But—and it's a big but—Scripture lays down another pattern of thought for us, not as a suggestion but as a command, one of true things and noble things, right things and pure things, lovely things and admirable things. Certainly envy does not fit any of those descriptions. To be a godly woman means learning not to give envy mind time. It means learning to be accepting and appreciative.

Being accepting means that you agree with God that he has made you as you are and placed you where you are. Being appreciative means agreeing with God that he has the right to make us all different, to make all our circumstances different, and that this is good.

"It was never God's intention for His children to look alike or embrace identical lifestyles. Look at the natural world He created. What variety! The buzzard and the butterfly . . . the dog and the deer . . . the zinnia and the orchid . . . the wriggling minnow and the sleek shark. . . . Variety honors God, predictability and mediocrity bore Him."[2]

As we put off envy and put on acceptance and appreciation, there are several areas where we must practice this discipline.

PEOPLE

PERSONALITIES

We have to accept and appreciate the different talents among God's children. We're gifted as we are so all the bases get covered. Many think they would like the up-front gifts, those of teaching and singing and leading. I'm convinced, however, that the church moves forward through the ministry of the quieter, more private gifts of encouraging and helping, the abilities practiced one to one in daily living situations. Up-front guys—and I consider myself one of them—are good for occasional things, be it Sunday sermons or annual retreats or books, but the daily gifts are good every minute of every day.

FINANCES

We have to accept and appreciate the differences in finances within the body of Christ. Again God distributes wealth as he wills. No matter where we are on the money scale, God has special things for us to learn, special ways for us to serve, either through giving or receiving.

Yeah, most of us think, *and I'd rather be on the learning-through-giving side. It's less embarrassing and somehow seems more American.* But there are lessons that cannot be learned on the giving side.

"I don't know if any of you have ever lived in poverty," says novelist Tracie Peterson, "but I have, and God never failed to provide for us, not once. Even when all our resources were exhausted and there was nothing in the cupboard and no money in my parents' pockets, even in those times, my folks taught me to share with those in need and to tithe and to seek God rather than material things."

EDUCATION

Another area where we need to learn to appreciate the differences among us is in educational opportunities, which frequently have little to do with our native intelligence and common sense. God's ability to use us is not governed by where we graduated or even if we graduated. It's governed by our heart's commitment and willingness to be used by him. Education may be a key that opens doors, but it's the wise and prayerful use of whatever resources we have that marks us as God's people.

Besides, he doesn't need all of us to start new ministries and try to win the world for Christ or found new companies and make millions. He needs us to talk to the people where we are, whether that's the assembly line because we never got to go to college or the board room because we went to an Ivy League school. He needs our finances dedicated to him whether we're the ones serving by giving or serving by receiving.

The differences between us are many and varied and wonderful. "Accept one another, then, just as Christ accepted you, in order to bring praise to God" (Rom. 15:7).

Accept one another in order to bring praise to God. In a world that is full of envy and competition, accepting one another becomes a testimony to the work of God in our hearts. "Accepting goes far beyond merely putting up with. It means receiving someone to ourselves without promise of a favorable reception in return."[3]

We're also asked to "be devoted to one another in brotherly love. Honor one another above yourselves" (Rom. 12:10). Honoring another means putting value on her, value above yourself.

When our son Chip was small, he received a teddy bear. This stuffed animal quickly became very special to Chip. He was not the most handsome bear on the market by any stretch of the imagination, but he became Chip's comfort, companion, and buddy. Through the years Teddy was valued, even when he lost an eye, even when he became moth-eaten in appearance. Even today Teddy is tucked away among Chip's special treasures.

Teddy was honored, valued, held in esteem. Would that we looked on others with the honor Chip assigned Teddy.

Paul wrote, "Rejoice with those who rejoice; mourn with those who mourn" (Rom. 12:15).

It's been my experience that people are more than willing to mourn with you when problems arise. Rarely do people compete to see whose life has the most sorrow in it. We sympathize, empathize, and weep, even when we don't know how to express our concern.

However, it takes a special person to rejoice with someone over a good thing, a special thing that will never be yours no matter how much you might wish it or how fervently you might pray for it. Your coworker gets the promotion you had hoped for. Her son gets accepted at the prestigious college while yours has to go to a state school. Her daughter makes the team, and yours gets cut. She loses ten pounds while you just gained five.

How can I rejoice with her? How can I not envy and resent the blessings to her and her family?

Only by learning to accept her and honor her in the name of Christ. Only by learning to value her above myself. Only by agreeing with God that he will give us—and deny us—what is best for us.

Our Personal Imperfections

The second area where we need to put on acceptance and appreciation is in regard to our own limitations. We are all flawed in personality and limited in our abilities. It goes with being human. It doesn't matter how much I may wish to be a soloist; I will never be one because of my musical limitations. It doesn't matter how much I might like the excitement of making a killing in the stock market; I don't understand even the basics of economics. It doesn't matter how much I might like to be there for people in trauma like friends who have special antennae for intercepting these situations; I'll still find out about the hospital stay or job loss weeks after the event.

In other words, in the immortal words of Popeye, "I yam what I yam."

Have you ever wondered why God didn't remove our imperfections when we believed? He could have if he'd wanted, and wouldn't that impress the world? Wouldn't people flock to Christ?

Sure they would, and all for the wrong reason. They wouldn't come as sinners in need of a Savior but as people seeking perfection and the good life.

"But we have this treasure in jars of clay to show that this all-surpassing power is from God and not from us" (2 Cor. 4:7).

God allows us to remain flawed jars of clay so that when we accomplish something, everyone knows it was by his strength and power, not ours. Our limitations are God's opportunities to show what he can do with less-than-perfect material. And he does quite a lot.

Have you ever thought what a miracle it is that the church has survived all these centuries, given the people that make it up? It is strictly the power of God.

And how about our local congregations? Mine survives in spite of having me in it, a sure sign of the grace of God at work.

When I talk about accepting ourselves as we are, I'm not saying we should overlook sin or that we shouldn't endeavor to develop our skills and talents. I'm saying we shouldn't waste time wishing God had made us someone else.

"For by the grace given me I say to every one of you: Do not think of yourself more highly than you ought, but rather think of yourself with sober judgment, in accordance with the measure of faith God has given you" (Rom. 12:3).

When I look at myself with sober judgment, I come to two conclusions—conclusions that also apply to you. There are abilities and disabilities mixed willy-nilly in me and in you. By the grace of God, he can use all of us in spite of the strange mix that we are—if we follow him.

PROCESS

A third area where we must learn appreciation and acceptance is in understanding that the Christian life is a process. We grow and develop slowly and at differing rates, just as children do physically.

I've heard new believers apologize for not knowing much about the Bible or not being able to explain some doctrine.

"I listen to Jane, and she knows so much!"

Of course she does. She's been a Christian for twenty-five years. She should know more, much more.

What the new believer doesn't appreciate is the shot in the arm that older, more mature Christians get from their enthusiasm for all the new things they are learning, their sense of freedom in their salvation. Their very babyhood is a blessing, proof that God is still mightily at work in the world.

When Peter encouraged the readers of his second letter to grow in the grace and knowledge of our Lord and Savior Jesus Christ, he was acknowledging that the Christian life is process. It's our responsibility not only to grow but also to be accepting of where we are in the process, to be certain not to stagnate, and to appreciate the growth of other believers, accepting their rate of growth rather than forcing ours on them.

When my sons were growing up, they were so different from each other. One never had a thought he didn't share, whether we wanted to hear it or not. The other never had a thought he did share, no matter how much we wanted to hear it. For reasons that should be obvious to anyone who was ever a mother or baby-sitter, the out-spoken son frequently got himself in trouble.

"It's not fair!" he'd complain. "You never yell at him!" And he'd point to his brother's room.

"We're not interested in what's fair," I'd answer. "We're interested in what's best for you, even if it seems like punishment."

When we envy someone, what we're saying is, "It's not fair! She's got something I want. Why can't I have it too?"

I don't know why you can't have it too. I don't know why a God of miracles chooses not to work those miracles more often on our behalf. But I do know that as I was interested in what was best for my sons, no matter how they saw it, how much more is God interested in what is best for us, no matter how we misunderstand him.

We see what we want. God sees what we need.

We see what we think will make us happy. God sees what he knows will make us content.

We yearn for what seems good. God offers us what is best.

We plead for the good things in life. God asks us to agree that he is enough.

"I can now recognize when negative traits are brewing in my gut and stop them the only way they are meant to be stopped—by focusing on the Lord instead of the world," says novelist Nancy Moser. "True contentment equals a focus on God."

And a focus on God equals agreeing with him even when we don't understand why he's not providing as we'd like.

QUESTIONS, QUESTIONS

1. What things could make you envious? What can you do to overcome the possible sin?

Envy

2. What action followed envy in the following stories? How are these stories warnings to us?
   Joseph and his brothers: Genesis 37:12–36
   Saul and David: 1 Samuel 18–19
   Jesus: Matthew 17–18
3. Read Titus 3:3–8. What does Titus expect to replace envy and by what power?
4. Read Proverbs 27:7. What do we learn about the damage that jealousy (envy in the KJV) can do?

Chapter 8

Greed

*There are two ways to get enough. One is to accumulate
more and more. The other is to desire less.*

—G. K. Chesterton

I don't know about you, but malls make me greedy.

Every time I go to a mall, I suddenly need things I didn't even
know existed fifteen minutes ago. I had been very contented with my
house, my wardrobe, Chuck's stuff, but suddenly, nothing's satisfac-
tory any more. My house needs refurbishing. My wardrobe needs a
complete overhaul. And Chuck's things!

My biggest area of sudden cravings is in the linens department. I
think it's the colors and the patterns. All those comforters. All those
matching sheets and pillowcases. All those soft towels. All those
pretty shower curtains.

Greed

I remember when sheets were white and a white sale was just that: a sale for white sheets. I remember when we all had chenille bedspreads of a single color, or if you were a boy, corduroy bedspreads of a single color. I remember when shower curtains were serviceable, not decorator statements. I remember when the glass on the sink was a glass.

"Be careful not to drop that, Gayle. It'll break," was as much a bathroom warning as, "Don't get anything electrical near the water."

But now the linens department in a big store is a sensory delight. There are easily three to five comforters that I love and now need, regardless of the fact that I already have all the beds at home perfectly well covered, and not with single-color corduroy. Just how many comforters can one person use, especially if the colors require painting the room every time you change the bedding?

It used to be that you changed bedspreads summer and winter (if you were well-off) because of the temperature variations. Now, with climate-controlled homes, there's not even the excuse of summer to buy another quilt. If you come right down to it, there's rarely an excuse to buy the first comforter if you use yours like we use ours. You pull it up each morning to make the bed and push it down each night because it's too warm in the house ever to need it.

But it's beautiful!

Ah, greed, that great old American emotion.

I see it!

I want it!

I need it!

I MUST have it!

The Bible is full of stories of people who wanted more and wanted it right now.

Eve wanted more and ate the fruit offered by the serpent. She was thrown out of the garden for her sin.

Jacob wanted more and tricked his father into giving him the birthright that should have been his brother's. He had to flee into exile for twenty years.

David wanted more when he saw and took Bathsheba. He reaped a dreadful whirlwind in his family as a result of this sin: the death of the son of his union with Bathsheba, the rebellious effort of Absalom to wrest the throne from David, and the serious problems of his other children.

Solomon wanted more and found that absolute power does corrupt absolutely as he took hundreds of wives and concubines and lowered himself to worship idols.

Our greed rarely reaches the extremes of these biblical characters. After all, our lives are hardly the stuff of epics. We're regular people living regular lives, but if we're not careful, on our own small scale, we can do ourselves plenty of damage, especially if we forget that greed doesn't always refer to money and things. We can be greedy for position and prestige as well as possessions.

When I taught junior high, there was a troubled boy in one seventh-grade class. Richard was an intelligent kid, but because of behavior problems and a poor home life, he'd never learned any disciplines. As a result he was in the lower academic classes and resented it immensely.

"I belong in the top class with all those smart dudes. I hate 'em but I'm as smart as any of them. Put me up there," he demanded regularly of the principal.

Finally he got himself in so much disciplinary trouble in the lower classes that in desperation the principal put him in the top section, which happened to be one of my English classes. The reasoning was that Richard didn't know these kids very well and so couldn't lead them around by the nose as easily as he had the kids in his regular classes. Also the gifted kids tended to be obedient, and maybe, just maybe, they'd be an example. Maybe, just maybe—if Richard were as smart as he always contended—he'd learn something, and not all of it would be academics.

The first day or two Richard was delighted to be in the best classes. He strutted down the hall, feeling great pride in his new prestigious position. Then he made some truly frightening discoveries. These kids listened. They were polite and respectful, especially in contrast to Richard. They applied themselves in class. They did their homework. In short, having the position at the top wasn't all he'd imagined. He'd thought to impress everyone, thought he'd be king of the hill, thought he'd teach these nerdy geniuses a thing or two.

He found out that mere greed for position isn't enough, and it was a painful, humiliating lesson.

Whether we're covetous of things, money, position, or recognition, the difficulties we cause ourselves are much the same. Paul writes to his young friend Timothy in terms of money, but the brush of application can be applied in broad strokes.

"People who want to get rich fall into temptation and a trap and into many foolish and harmful desires that plunge men into ruin and destruction. For the love of money is a root of all kinds of evil. Some people, eager for money, have wandered from the faith and pierced themselves with many griefs. But you, man of God, flee from all this, and pursue righteousness, godliness, faith, love, endurance and gentleness" (1 Tim. 6:9–11).

The most frightening line in this passage, at least to me, is: *Some people, eager for money, have wandered from the faith and pierced themselves with many griefs.* I guess this line stands out because I've seen

Christians who have lived out this verse, and they and their families have suffered everything from separation and divorce to ungrateful or estranged kids to ruined health to no true friends.

I'm not saying that no one should become successful and rich or that the Richards of this world are doomed to stay where they began. Not at all. Gifted people will always achieve if they try, and the Bible is full of wealthy achievers. The patriarchs were very wealthy. David and Solomon were wealthy beyond our imaginings. Job was wealthy before and after his loss of everything.

The New Testament is full of wealthy people too. Some were like the rich young ruler who couldn't see beyond his money, and some were like Joseph of Arimathea who used his wealth to provide a burial place for Christ, and Lydia who used her money to provide hospitality for Paul and his missionary party.

God never condemned any of the rich for their wealth alone. Perhaps he said some pretty sharp things about the way the wealth was wielded, but the wealth itself was not the problem. Nor are riches alone an automatic uh-oh to God today. The question remains always: Is the wealth producing greed or being used to honor God? Is it causing you to wander from the faith or are you a person who remembers it's always Christ first and ambition, success, position, and prestige a distant second. Is it pulling you from God, or are you a person who pursues righteousness, godliness, faith, love, endurance, and gentleness?

"Command those who are rich in this present world not to be arrogant nor to put their hope in wealth, which is so uncertain, but to put their hope in God, who richly provides us with everything for our enjoyment. Command them to do good, to be rich in good deeds, and to be generous and willing to share. In this way they will lay up treasure for themselves as a firm foundation for the coming age, so that they may take hold of the life that is truly life" (1 Tim. 6:17–19).

"When we ask ourselves why, in any given situation, we committed a sin, the answer is usually one of two things. Either we wanted to obtain something we didn't have, or we feared losing something we had."[1]

I've noticed, as I'm sure you have, that one of the major characteristics of greed is selfishness. I need another outfit. I want a larger house. I want a more prestigious address. I deserve a splashy vacation. I want the biggest diamond available. I want new comforters.

Keeping selfishness company is pride. I will look nicer than anyone in my new outfit. I will have the best house. I will impress everyone when they see where I live. I will win bragging rights on the best trip, hands down. I will make Connie's ring look so bad. I will have the prettiest bedrooms around.

We Ropers live at the eastern edge of Lancaster County, Pennsylvania, home of one of the largest and most well-known Amish communities. They are a fascinating people with their ardent refusal to be part of what we consider the real world.

One of their cardinal tenets is community and family over self. The severe dress code and the uniform hairstyles are designed to diminish self. Compliments are rare because they encourage self-appreciation. Everything is designed to prevent the encroachment of the materialism that so consumes the rest of the country.

"Many modern habits signal pride in Amish eyes. Jewelry, wristwatches, fashionable clothing and personal photographs accentuate individuality and call attention to one's self. . . . Dress in modern life is used to express individuality and social status. It is the tool of individualism. By sharp contrast, ethnic dress in Amish life is a badge of group allegiance and identity."[2]

For several years I had a young woman who came biweekly to help with the housework so I had more time for writing. She was Plain, wearing the prayer *kapp* and the caped dress that many Plain women wear. (*Plain* is a very broad term, including Mennonites who often look no different from you or me.) Though her parents were house Amish, Ruthie no longer considered herself Amish because, as she told me, "I believe in salvation by grace, not works." In her freedom from strict Amish teachings, Ruthie allowed herself to wear a variety of colors instead of the traditional royal blue and purple or emerald green. She'd wear a brown dress with a beige apron or a navy dress with a pale blue apron.

I suspected she'd never consider wearing red, one of my favorite colors, because it was either too wild or the sign of a fallen woman. But what about other colors?

One day I asked, "Ruthie, would you ever consider wearing pink or yellow or any bright, light color like that? After all, God created those colors, and we see them in such beauty in flowers."

She looked at me aghast. "Oh, no. I'd never wear anything like that because it would call attention to me, and that would be wrong."

It was not a matter of whether she liked or disliked those colors, nor was it a matter of whether they would look good on her. It was a matter of denying herself for the sake of God and community.

Ruthie and her community can make a strong argument from Scripture on yielding self, pride, and greed.

"Do nothing out of selfish ambition or vain conceit, but in humility consider others better than yourselves. Each of you should look not only to your own interests, but also to the interests of others" (Phil. 2:3–4).

"Humility is the hallmark of Amish ideals. Mild and modest personalities are esteemed. Patience, waiting, yielding to others and a gentle chuckle are the marks of maturity. Modern culture, by contrast, stresses individual achievement, competition, assertiveness, self-fulfillment, individual rights and personal choice. While other Americans work hard to 'find themselves,' the Amish work hard to 'lose themselves' in the goals and activities of their community. Modern culture applauds independence, freedom and egoism, while the Amish cheer conformity, modesty and humility."³

While most of us would agree with the Amish principles of strong family and church, we would not agree with the extreme patterns they follow to achieve their goals. Rather, we would come down on the side of balance. Of course, in many ways, it's easier to have the rules spelled out clearly than it is to think through an issue to a point of balance, but I much prefer the freedom of thought to the comfort of law.

When our guys were small, TV ads for Christmas began earlier and earlier every year. It seemed that Labor Day had barely passed when they started running from the living room shouting, "I know what I want for Christmas! I want—" And they'd name whatever had just been shown in a clever ad that made it seem larger and much more interesting than the toy actually was.

After many, too many, rushes to tell me their latest heart's desire, which, in total, we could never have afforded, I laid down what became an ironclad rule: no telling us what they wanted for Christmas until after Thanksgiving.

There was balance there. There wasn't the extreme of law: no TV. Nor was it the other extreme of responding to every childish whim and encouraging greed and selfishness. The kids could still watch appropriate TV, still think about Christmas and its possibilities, but they were no longer consumed by it. By the time Thanksgiving arrived, they weren't entranced by the ads any more because they'd been watching them for quite some time now. When they told us what they wanted, they actually told us what they wanted, not what some clever admeister had convinced them was wonderful.

Balance.

Self-discipline.

Delayed gratification.

"The meaning of earthly existence lies not, as we have grown used to thinking, in prospering, but . . . in the development of the soul."[4]

Yes, Lord, we say. I'm learning the need to develop my soul more clearly every day. But how do we teach this truth to our children? So much of what they hear is buy, buy, buy, get, get, get. How can we counter this siren song of our culture?

I did a very informal survey, asking a variety of friends what concrete things they did to help keep their children from being consumed by materialism. I wanted practical suggestions anyone could use. Of course, not all will work for all of us, but I pray some might and that others will spark some original ideas of your own.

"The best thing we've done to stave off greed is to be poor," writes Deborah Raney. "Seriously! When our kids were growing up, we were a one-income family (and not a very big income at that). Just ordering a pizza was a major treat that required a windfall of some sort to finance it. It made the kids UTTERLY grateful for any steak they might have."

Deb continued, "As far as making being practical for people who aren't poor, when I was growing up, my parents 'pretended' we were poor, though I realize now we were far from it. While our friends were getting radios and bicycles for Christmas, we were thrilled with our coloring books and board games because we didn't get those every trip to the grocery store like some of our friends did."

"I think we have missed the boat with our children in teaching them the joy of waiting for something," said Rachel Williams, wife of the director of the Mount Hermon Christian Conference Center. "Because I was raised in a family that was rather poor, I knew what it was like not to have nice things and to have only handmade clothing until I was twelve or so. I have an ingrained sense that I don't want my kids to have to live like that, so I've gone out of my way at times to fulfill their desires for clothing and other things. Not good, and I still have to be reined in from time to time by my dear, practical husband.

"Because I recognize my tendency," Rachel continued, "I've begun encouraging our youngest daughter (who is still at home) to cover her own expenses, making her pay for the things she 'wants,' and we handle the things she 'needs.' That helps slow her down some. Our older daughter, now that she's in college and using her own savings to live, is much more careful with her spending than she used to be."

"When our girls were small," Patsy Green, wife of one of our pastors and an excellent Bible study teacher, said, "we limited the amount of TV they were allowed to watch for a variety of reasons. They were more willing to be creative about games and playtime, less demanding of the latest toy or fad."

"When our daughter asks for something," said our daughter-in-law Cindy, "our usual answer is, 'Wait a while.' If she still wants the item when her birthday comes around or Christmas or we have some extra funds, then we know we're buying her something she truly wants, not some fad she heard mentioned at school or on TV."

"Every Christmas we have a giving tree at our restaurant," said Debby, who with her husband Mike co-owns one of my favorite eateries, The Country Garden. "The goods collected are donated to a local street mission. We make certain we take our children with us when we take the gifts. We want them to see how blessed they are and how hard life is for some folks."

"I remember very clearly," said our older son Chip, "one Christmas when I asked Dad why we didn't have as many presents as some of my friends. 'Because we give regularly to the Lord and they probably don't,' he answered. It made an enormous impression on me, originally making me sort of angry at God for ruining my Christmas, but now I respect it immensely."

"One of the ways we helped our kids avoid greed," Tracie Peterson said, "was to teach them early on that the things they were given were theirs to do with as they pleased. We reminded them that things were only things. They didn't have feelings or hearts or souls. However, we did, and if we let 'things take over,' we would soon begin to act without feeling, heart, or soul. As a result, from the time they were little, they would practice giving whenever the urge came upon them, and we always encouraged it. I've watched my son give away brand new toys to kids he deemed needier than himself. He rarely shows greed because he has a pretty clear vision that the things of this earth are just temporary and we are just their temporary keepers."

"We've begun a tradition in our house of giving to Heifer Project in the names of our children and grandchildren," said my friend Suzanne. "We don't do this in place of traditional Christmas gifts, but the card telling each person that a sheep or goat or flock of chicks has been given in his or her name is the first gift we give on Christmas Day. We want everyone to appreciate the needs of the body of Christ around the world even as they enjoy our plenty."

"Whenever we received extra income as in a bonus," our friend Harry said, "we sat down with our kids and discussed where we could give a portion of this special money. They knew we gave regularly to church and that that money wasn't open to discussion. But the disbursement of special monies was a family decision."

Greed

"It seems to me," said Patsy Green, "that every child has one birthday when greed takes over. She may be five or six or fifteen or sixteen. 'I only got three presents!' or, 'I don't like anything I got!' or, 'That's it? There isn't any more?' That's when you take the child aside and have a heart-to-heart about attitude and gratitude. You have to catch that nasty mind-set right away, or it grows."

"I remember when we were first married," said Paul, a close friend. "I was still in school, and we had no money. Our furniture consisted of aluminum lawn chairs. At the end of the week, we'd have fifty cents, not even enough to order a pizza. We'd go around to the other student apartments, and we'd pool our money until we could afford a pizza. Then we'd all share. Those hard times are some of our best memories. I remind myself of that so I don't automatically bail our married kids out of financial binds. Let them learn together. Let them build memories."

"My parents were givers," said Jean, a member of my Prayer Board. "I learned about giving because they modeled it for us kids. They never considered their money theirs but the Lord's. That made giving it away easy and fun. They were the epitome of cheerful givers. We're trying to show the same principles to our children."

"Our oldest daughter went on a short-term missions trip," said Rachel Williams. "She spent five weeks in Ivory Coast living in the bush with the Yacuba Tribe, an unreached tribe. She came back very sensitive to waste and unnecessary accumulation of things. In fact, she has challenged us in our choices in these areas. I do believe that missions trips are a good way to teach reality in finances."

HOW TO GREED-PROOF YOUR KIDS

1. Establish clear spending limits for clothes and toys, and communicate the limits to the kids. Let them know that when that limit is reached, that's it until next season.

2. Discuss who should receive any extra giving that comes from bonuses, raises, etc. with the kids. It's important they know you take giving seriously.

3. Teach them to give a portion of any monies they earn.

4. If they desire big-money items, offer to split the cost with them. If they have to earn half the price, they will not buy on impulse or be as swayed by fads, and they will appreciate the item's worth. Hopefully all these things translate into their taking care of the item.

5. At Christmas buy with them gifts for the less fortunate and deliver them with the kids. Project Angel Tree sponsored by Prison Fellowship is a good way to do this.

6. Support a child through Compassion International or World Vision. Teens of a friend did this after the parents took them to a Christian music festival where the musicians pitched Compassion.

7. Encourage summer missions trips. Let the kids see how the rest of the world lives.

8. From the time they are little, let the kids know that every gum machine or device with a quarter slot does not get fed. Also every trip to the mall does not mean a purchase for them.

9. Don't give them a credit card until they are old enough to handle it, and the age varies with each child. Don't cover debts you did not authorize.

10. Let teen drivers buy their own insurance or be responsible for any increases in the insurance that occur because of their driving mistakes.

11. Encourage teens to hold summer or part-time jobs, being careful these don't take the teens from church and youth activities.

12. When a possession is damaged or ruined, especially through the carelessness of the child, do not automatically or immediately replace it, no matter how dramatic or heartfelt the tears. Hold the child accountable.

13. Model a moderate spending pattern before them. Do not spend above your income.

14. Model giving before them—giving to church, to missions, to special projects and charities, and to individuals in need.

QUESTIONS, QUESTIONS

1. What things tend to make you greedy, and how can you counter them?

2. Read 1 Chronicles 29:14, 16. What do we learn about our possessions here? What does this teach us about greed?

3. Read 2 Corinthians 8:9. How does this example of Christ translate into our lives?

4. Read Philippians 4:18–19. How does Paul describe the gift he has received, and how does it tie into God's provision for us?

5. Read Luke 21:1–4. What does this story teach you about giving?

Chapter 9

Disappointment

A contented person is one who can enjoy the scenery on a detour.
                                                              —Anonymous

From the time my father was a kid, he wanted to be a professional musician. To that end he graduated from college at twenty with a degree in music.

One of the family legends concerns a men's quartet that Dad wanted to sing with. The group had an opening, and Dad tried out. The group wore green blazers, white slacks, and green and white spectator shoes. Dad was able to get hold of the blazer and the slacks, but the shoes were just beyond his very tight budget, it being the Depression. So great was his determination to sing with this group that he took his one good pair of dress shoes and painted them green and white.

Disappointment

He made the group.

As a young man Dad organized his own big band. It was the days of Tommy and Jimmy Dorsey, Harry James, Glenn Miller, Benny Goodman, and the other great bands. Chuck Gordon and his Orchestra played throughout the Northeast. I remember as a child the rehearsals in our living room, the men crowded together in the small space, playing, laughing, having a wonderful time while the wives sat in the kitchen with my mother, talking and gossiping. I remember Dad writing out all the music arrangements by hand with a fountain pen, spending hours on a single song as he wrote out each instrument's part.

Some of Dad's biggest moments came during World War II when many of the big names weren't available stateside. Bands like Dad's filled in at top venues, providing excellent music in spite of the lack of national recognition of their names. One of Dad's biggest moments was playing Steel Pier in Atlantic City.

But with the end of the war came the end of the big band era. The huge names were able to survive, though just barely, but the yeoman musicians were not. The finances of big bands were part of the reason for their demise. The rise of individual singers like Frank Sinatra and Frankie Laine made paying for sixteen or more musicians obsolete. All that was now needed was a piano player and a singer. And public taste had changed, as it always does.

As a result, what my father had hoped would be his vocation became an avocation while he pursued various careers to provide money for us to live. He eventually settled on teaching, which he did well, earning a prestigious New Jersey Teacher of the Year Award.

But there was always a touch of disappointment over the death of his dream. Through circumstances over which he had no control, he could not be what he had worked so hard to become, what his heart yearned to be. Teaching junior-high kids, no matter how well he did it, just wasn't the same as standing before an audience, playing his trumpet, his musicians behind him.

Dad is far from the only person who is disappointed with things beyond his control. Many experience the grinding emotions of seeing a dream die.

Scripture tells us of a similar occurrence involving Naomi.

A wife and mother of two sons, Naomi had a life that matched her name, which means "pleasant." Even when a famine struck Judah, and she and Elimelech took their sons into Moab, she still had those she loved around her. Life was still pleasant.

While the family lived in Moab, the sons, Mahlon and Kilion, grew to maturity. Then the first tragedy struck Naomi. Elimelech died. We don't know why he died or how old he was, but suddenly instead of being a loved wife, Naomi was a widow in a foreign land.

Mahlon and Kilion married Moabite women, so for a time Naomi still had the consolation of family, though it wasn't the same as the comfort of Elimelech's arms about her. Then Mahlon and Kilion died also. We don't know how they died any more than we know how their father died, but we can imagine Naomi's pain as she buried her sons.

It isn't supposed to be this way, she undoubtedly thought. *Children bury their parents, not the other way around. They are supposed to live long, have many children, and bury me.*

Now she was not only a widow in a foreign land. She was alone, except for her daughters-in-law. There were no grandchildren to carry on the family line. There were only Orpah and Ruth, the Moabites.

"The Lord's hand has gone out against me," Naomi wept as sorrow rolled through her.

Disappointment

When she heard that the famine in Judah was finally over, she decided to go back to her former home in Bethlehem. Why not? She'd lost everything she valued. She might as well go back and at least have the comfort of the familiar.

Naomi said to her daughters-in-law, "Go back to your mothers' homes. You need to find other husbands. Since I can't give them to you, I encourage you to go home."

Both the young women cried and kissed Naomi and said, "We'll go back with you to your people."

The willingness of these young women to go to Judah with Naomi says much about what they thought of their mother-in-law, which in turn says much about the tenor of this family. The respect and affection of Orpah and Ruth must be a mere shadow of the love Naomi had shared with Elimelech and their sons. How incredibly painful would have been the loss of that love and support.

In the end Orpah did return to her mother's home, but Ruth followed Naomi to Bethlehem. When the two women arrived in this small town, the people were shocked.

"Can this be Naomi?" they asked.

"Don't call me Naomi," she answered, overwhelmed by emotion. "Call me Mara (which means bitter) because the Almighty has made my life very bitter. I went away full, but the Lord has brought me back empty."

Certainly we understand Naomi's grief. Life had not gone according to plan, as life frequently doesn't.

A given: life will guarantee you adversity. The only question is how to deal with it.

—Christian Hagaseth II

A few weeks ago a pastor friend received a call from the local police, asking him to go with them to the home of a family whose son had just been killed in a terrible accident. When they arrived at the house, they found a family already reeling from the mother's struggle with cancer and the death seven months earlier of the father. It was all the two surviving teenage children could do to take in the latest tragedy.

"May I pray with you?" the pastor asked. "I'd like to ask God to give you his comfort and strength."

The mother stared at him with steely eyes. "We will not pray."

"You don't have to if you don't want to," the pastor said, misunderstanding her. "I'll pray, and you just listen. You can pray along in your heart."

"No," said the mother, bitterness filling her voice. "We will not pray, you will not pray, no one will pray in this house."

"I've gone many times with the police to give comfort when they report a tragedy," the pastor said later. "This was the first time anyone has refused to let me pray. And I must say that humanly speaking, I understand the woman's bitterness."

Bitterness because of circumstances.

But there's a difference between Naomi's story and the one the pastor related, and the difference has to do with Naomi's faith. Even in the midst of her great despair, Naomi recognized God as the Sovereign. She may not have liked what he had allowed, but she knew him as the true God, even when she said things like, "The Almighty has brought misfortune upon me."

As the story of Naomi progresses and becomes the love story of Ruth and Boaz, in the background is Naomi telling Ruth what to do according to Jewish law and tradition. When Naomi learns how kind Boaz has been to Ruth, she says, "The Lord bless him! The

Lord has not stopped showing his kindness to the living and the dead."

Always, in spite of the bitterness, there is in Naomi a recognition of God in control. When Ruth and Boaz marry and have a son, Naomi finds joy in the child and in the knowledge that God has not abandoned her. He was working his plan, and all Naomi's detours and tears were part of that plan that made this child the grandfather of King David.

"Praise be to the Lord," cry the women of Bethlehem after the child is born.

"Then Naomi took the child, laid him in her lap and cared for him" (Ruth 4:16).

She is no longer Mara but once again Naomi because she clung to Jehovah God even through the bitterness.

Sometimes it's not circumstances but people who disappoint us. Haven't we all had times when we were hurt or unpleasantly surprised by something someone has said or done? I wonder sometimes why we are so surprised. It's not like people have proved themselves trustworthy in the past. People always disappoint. How can it be otherwise in an imperfect world peopled with imperfect individuals? Yet we continue to get taken unawares, especially by those closest to us.

I don't think the unexpectedness of our hurt is a bad thing. It's good we trust. It's good we love. It's good we give people the benefit of the doubt. These positive traits are all modeled for us by God our Father as he deals with us, his children. He knows we will disappoint him, yet he's always there for us, offering us the option to do better. And many times, because of his love and care, we do make better choices. When we trust people, we're just offering the same options, and many times the people we love make better choices too.

But sometimes they don't. Few things wound as intensely as when someone we love or respect disappoints us either on purpose or inadvertently.

Joseph was one who knew this betrayal all too well. First his father, in the name of loving him, set him up as the favorite with preferential treatment and extraordinary gifts like the glorious coat of many colors. Jacob may have meant well, but he paved the way for his older ten sons to resent his eleventh.

When Jacob sent Joseph with a message for the brothers who were out with the flocks, the stage for tragedy had been well set. When the brothers saw Joseph approaching, they said, "Here comes the dreamer. Come now, let's kill him, throw his body in a cistern, and say a wild animal ate him."

Reuben, the oldest of the brothers, tried to prevent the murder. "Let's not shed blood. Let's just throw him into a cistern, but not lay a hand on him."

The brothers agreed. Joseph would be gone. That was all that counted. Secretly Rueben planned to return later and free him.

When Joseph reached them, the brothers stripped him and threw him into the cistern. Then they sat down to eat. There is a hardheartedness and callousness about this action that cuts through any sympathy we might have felt for the brothers as their father shunted them aside in favor of Joseph.

When a caravan came by loaded with spices and riches to trade in Egypt, the brothers decided that they'd sell Joseph instead of commiting fratricide. This time it was Judah, Jacob's fourth son, who stepped up to "protect" Joseph.

"Come," said Judah. "Let's sell him to the Ishmaelites and not lay our hands on him; after all, he is our brother, our own flesh and blood."

And so his brothers, the very ones Joseph should have been able to depend on for love and protection, his own flesh and blood, sold him as a slave. Out of jealousy. Out of spite. Out of fear for their position before their father. Talk about betrayal!

Carleen had a similar experience, though it wasn't her brothers who betrayed her. It was her husband.

Carleen loved Tim with all her heart. He was all she'd ever prayed for in a husband: kind, loving, supportive, godly. It was a bonus that he was also handsome. Tim was a Christian school principal well respected in Christian education circles, in their church, and in the community. He was a wonderful father to their three young children.

One evening Carleen found Tim at the front door with a suitcase. Trying to think what convention she had forgotten he was attending, she said, "Where are you going?" She smiled and hugged him. "I can't remember."

"That's because I didn't tell you," he said, taking her by the arms and setting her away from him. "I'm leaving."

"Obviously," she said. "But where are you going and when will you be back? Don't forget Timmy's game Friday."

"No," he said. "I mean, I'm leaving, as in not coming back. Ever." Carleen stared at him. "What?"

"I can't live with a goody-goody like you any more. I need my freedom." And he was gone.

Several days later after she recovered enough from the initial shock of Tim's desertion to begin thinking again, Carleen started putting clues together. Multiple late-night meetings. A growing coolness toward her that she had blamed on harried schedules. A subtle withdrawal from his involvement with their kids and at church. And most scary, messages appearing on the computer advertising porn sites, messages that Tim had previously convinced her everyone got. In desperation she checked Tim's E-mail, and the tale was told.

When Carleen discovered the girlfriend whom he had met online at a porn chat room, it was now no great surprise. Nor was the fact that Tim's new address was the same as this woman's. Tim had turned his back completely on God and all things Christian, including his loving family.

Within an unbelievably short period of time, Tim lost his job for character reasons, the children lost a godly father, and Carleen lost the man she had deeply loved and depended on to seek her best.

"But in the blackest of nights, I knew God was there," she told friends who formed a hedge of prayer around her and the children. "When the agony was a consuming fire, I knew his presence."

Joseph's experience was similar to Carleen's; in the darkest night he knew God was there too. Years later, when there was a famine in Israel and the brothers came to Egypt to purchase grain, they did not recognize the authoritative figure standing before them as their younger brother. When Joseph finally revealed who he was and asked if his father still lived, the brothers were unable to answer him, they were so terrified.

Joseph reassured his brothers and protected them and his father, giving them a place to live in Egypt. All was well until Jacob died, and again the brothers feared Joseph.

"What if Joseph holds a grudge against us and pays us back for all the wrongs we did him?" they asked one another. They came and threw themselves at Joseph's feet saying, "We are your servants."

"Don't be afraid," Joseph said. "Am I in the place of God? You intended to harm me, but God intended it for good to accomplish what is now being done."

Disappointment

In other words, through the darkest of Joseph's nights, God was working. When things seemed blackest to Joseph, God knew what he was doing. He was working all things for good, refining Joseph from a bragging boy to a man capable of being second only to Pharaoh.

And God is doing the same for Carleen. In the deepest, most dismal nights of her life, God was there. Tim's turning from God was an act of defiance, a fist shaken in the face of the Most High, but God will do great things for Carleen in spite of this major disruption of her life, her future, because he is her loving Father.

Sometimes we tend to think that God has one plan for our lives, and when something happens to throw a monkey wrench into the works, we will never be useful to God again. At best we have now secondary roles in the great spiritual battles being played out upon life's stage.

Not so at all! How dare we so limit God! Just because I can't see what he's going to do in Carleen's future doesn't mean God's stymied.

The brothers meant their action for evil, and Joseph must have wondered many times if his life would ever amount to anything, but God came through beyond Joseph's wildest imaginings. So will God come through for Carleen.

It's all a matter of hanging on through the darkness and giving the disappointment and pain to God. He will make something wonderful beyond our imaginings from the ashes of our dreams.

"Then you will know that I am the LORD;
   those who hope in me will not be disappointed."

(Isa. 49:23b)

Sometimes we find ourselves so disappointed, so harried, so pressed to the wall that it is all we can do to hang on to our faith.

Such was the experience of a father who had a seriously ill son. The boy could not speak. He was stricken with convulsions that had caused him injury when he fell into fire or water. When he convulsed, he became rigid, foamed at the mouth, and gnashed himself with his teeth.

In utter desperation the father brought his child to the disciples for healing, but the disciples could do nothing. What wracking disappointment must have torn through the man.

Then Jesus approached, and the father spoke to him.

"Teacher, I brought you my son."

I can imagine the mingling emotions this man must have felt as he held his son out to the One they said was the Messiah. Love and sorrow for his boy must have ripped his heart, causing his very soul to bleed. And the helplessness! The fear for the boy's safety, for the future.

"How long has he been like this?" Jesus asked.

"From childhood. If you can do anything, take pity on us and help us."

If you can?

I wonder how many others besides the disciples this father had already turned to for help. Had he approached other healers? Other gods? We don't know whether the man was Jewish or Roman or perhaps another nationality. We just know that no one had been able to do a thing for his son.

I find it reasonable that this father is skeptical. *If* you can. After all, no one else could work the needed miracle in spite of claims made. *If* you can. That way, if Jesus can't, then the disappointment isn't killing. It's just another hurt in a long line of searing hurts, another day in endless years of torment. Tomorrow or maybe the day after, when he has his courage and strength back, he'll look for another possible cure. *If* you can.

"If you can?" said Jesus, going right to the nub of the issue. "Everything is possible for him who believes."

What a promise to a heart-weary father! Everything is possible! Everything includes healing. Everything includes a son with alert eyes, a clear mind, a healthy body. Hope surges.

But there's a catch. Everything is possible *for him who believes.*

Immediately the boy's father exclaimed, "I do believe; help me overcome unbelief!"

Have you been in situations where belief and unbelief wrestled within you? *Sure,* you said to yourself, *I know God can do anything. After all, he's God. But will he? And why should he do this for me?*

We cut ourselves on this two-edged dilemma because God doesn't grant every request we make, even when we ask out of disappointment and desperation like this father. Countless parents have gone to God on behalf of their suffering children and not seen the healing this man saw. They come to live with belief laced with unbelief.

But we hang on through our disappointment, clinging to our belief in the goodness of God in spite of the unbelief and skepticism caused by his denial of our request. Some days we fear we need longer fingernails or we won't be able to hang on any more. We feel like a character from an old-time movie dangling from a windowsill or flagpole.

But we do hang on, and we hang on because as Peter said, "Lord, to whom shall we go? You have the words of eternal life" (John 6:68).

And God also has the long view. We have only the pain of today often experienced in the impenetrable fog of confusion. But because he is sovereign and knows where this disappointment will lead, we hang on until we do more than merely survive, merely manage. Eventually we will find ease, rest, contentment.

"And now, my dear," wrote Harriet Beecher Stowe to her best friend in 1836, "perhaps the wonder to you, as to me, is how this momentous crisis in the life of such a wisp of nerves as myself has been transacted so quietly. My dear, it is a wonder to myself. I am tranquil, quiet and happy. I look only on the present, and leave the future with Him who has hitherto been so kind to me. 'Take no thought of the morrow' is my motto, and my comfort is to rest on Him."[1]

But what about the promise that all things are to happen for good for God's people (Rom. 8:28)? Why are our lives laced with so many bitter experiences if God wants everything to benefit us? How does this all make sense?

It's a matter of how you define *good.* If good is health, money, and ease, then life is a hard experience that seems to make a liar of God.

But if good is being conformed to the image of God, becoming Christlike, being made holy, then disappointments are but one of the refining techniques of the Master Jeweler. As we go through the crucible of disappointment, impurities in motive, character, and goals burn away. With the pure metal remaining, he fashions a beautiful piece that reflects himself to the world.

"If Thou, O God, had spared the strokes of Thy hammer, I should never have been formed to be an instrument for Thy use," wrote Madame Guyon.[2]

Contentment lives where we believe God through the disappointments he allows to come our way, knowing that in his goodness he is choosing for our best, painful though the hammer strokes may be.

QUESTIONS, QUESTIONS

1. What situation(s) have disappointed you enough to make you struggle with God?
2. Read Psalm 22:4–5. What are some of the situations where the fathers cried to God? How do these verses apply to you?
3. Read Romans 5:5–6. Why are we not disappointed?
4. Read Romans 3:23–24. How do we disappoint God? How is the situation rectified?
5. Read Philippians 3:10. What are Paul's three prayers? Which touches on this chapter and how?

Chapter 10

Loneliness

*Let the desolate soul take comfort from the fact that God is
just as present with His lonely children today as
He was with His Son.*
—J. Oswald Sanders

Jill, a single woman in her early thirties, slipped into the
Christmas Eve service late. The sanctuary was packed, and it was
standing room only. She moved away from the door, eyes on the
choir up front. She found a place against the back wall and settled in
to listen. When the number was over, she glanced around. To her
extreme distress, she realized she was standing next to her ex-
boyfriend and his new wife.

"It was a nightmare," Jill said. "Christmas Eve is always hard for
me in the best of circumstances because I know there will be no

special presents for me and no special hugs from that certain someone. So I was already struggling more than usual with loneliness. Then there stood Chad and Erin.

"After a moment of frozen panic, I turned my back on them and rushed out of church. I knew I was overreacting, but I couldn't help it. I ran to my car and drove back to my apartment as tears streamed down my face."

Jill grimaced. "It was so stupid. I didn't want Chad back. I didn't want to be Erin, married to him. But I did want to have someone who was mine. There they were, all rosy in the glow of their first Christmas, and there I was, alone." She paused and swallowed. "Some days being single is the pits."

No one likes being lonely.

"Being alone involves only physical separation, but being lonely includes both spiritual and psychological isolation. It produces a solitude of the heart, the feeling of being cut off from others."[1]

Author/speaker/counselor Georgia Shaffer, a single parent, spoke of the loneliness she felt when her only child went off to college. "I'll never again see him rush up the steps of that yellow school bus. I'll never sit with him, working on homework. I'll never have quite the same urgency to attend events at the local schools. I'll never read Bible stories to him like I used to." She sighed. "It's a whole new world for me, and it's lonely."

Journalist Patricia Johnson was widowed at a young age and left with three children to raise when her husband Tom died of cancer.

At the time of Tom's death, Pat wrote:

I'm crying again.
I miss Tom—
But more than that I miss the things that will never happen.

We'll never touch again.
We'll never love again.
We'll never look at each other knowing what the other is thinking.
We'll never lie beside each other just being there.
We'll never see our children grow up.
We'll never see our grandchildren.
We are no longer we—just me.
And I hate it!
I am so alone.

It would be easy to think that God doesn't understand loneliness. After all, he's God, and therefore he's above feelings like this.

But he does understand because Jesus was totally alone on the cross. His disciples had all fled, deserting him, denying him. Even God the Father turned his back when the sins of the world were placed upon Christ. Absolute aloneness.

So God does understand, and he has taken steps to ensure that we never need know such absolute aloneness. To this end he created in us two distinct connective needs, and meeting these needs slays or at least deeply wounds the scaly, fire-breathing, frightening dragon of loneliness. One need is for the companionship of people; the other is for a relationship with God himself.

THE COMPANIONSHIP OF PEOPLE

When Adam was naming all the beasts of field and the birds of the air, "for Adam no suitable helper was found" (Gen. 2:20). Both God and Adam recognized his need for human companionship.

"It is not good for the man to be alone," the Lord said. "I will make a helper suitable for him" (Gen. 2:18). And he made Eve.

Quite simply, from the beginning of time, people have needed people. When there aren't people close to us, people we love, people we enjoy, people we play with and disagree with and grow with, we feel the lack very deeply.

Solomon realized our human need for connection when he wrote,

"Two are better than one,
> because they have a good return for their work:
If one falls down,
> his friend can help him up.
But pity the man who falls
> and has no one to help him up!
Also, if two lie down together, they will keep warm.
> But how can one keep warm alone?
Though one may be overpowered,
> two can defend themselves.
A cord of three strands is not quickly broken." (Eccl. 4:9–12)

When I received the phone call that told us a baby boy was awaiting our adoption, I wanted to share that wonderful news. I quickly called Chuck at work and cried over the phone with him. Then I called my mother-in-law, and no one was home. I knew I couldn't reach my parents because they were both at work. I also knew I couldn't call other people until I'd told the grandparents. There I was with all this wonderful news I couldn't share. Talk about frustrating! I needed people to make my joy fuller.

David, in a psalm of rejoicing and praise, talks about God's connective provision for his people when he says that God "sets the lonely in families" (Ps. 68:6).

For some of us, that means the traditional family: husband, wife, 2.5 kids, a dog, and a cat. But for many of us, he doesn't set us in that kind of a family. He instead provides those we will love in alternative ways, often through the close ties of a local congregation.

"When you are trying to be less lonely, cultivate one relationship you feel comfortable with," suggests Georgia Shaffer. "Take a risk and invite someone to dinner or to go with you to a movie or out to lunch. If person A is unavailable, then ask person B. I've been single for years, and I've learned that reaching out and serving others distracts me from myself, my loneliness, my pain. I've also made some wonderful friends because I reached out."

The use of the phrase "one another" in the New Testament more than fifty times indicates how much emphasis God puts on our being there for one another as participants in the body of Christ. The good old American ideal of being independent isn't biblical. We are called to be dependent on God and interdependent within the church.

One evening at a church supper, I was bemoaning the problem I have with weight loss.

"It's such a lonely job," I said. "Just me and my unfriendly scale."

"It doesn't have to be lonely," said the woman across the table. "What do you think all those 'one another' verses are for? Get friends to pray and encourage you. 'Bear one another's burdens.' If this is your burden, get others involved on your behalf."

I have to admit that prior to that conversation, I had seen the one-another verses as emergency provisions. People are dying. Encourage them. Love them. People have fallen into gross sin. Confront them. Build them up. People in leadership have made a decision. Submit to them.

Now I saw the everyday possibilities in caring for one another. When we get involved in each other's lives in a healthy way, we offer ourselves. In that wonderful dichotomy, as we lose ourselves, we find ourselves. And we find friends.

People relationships come in layers, and we need to remember that fact. Not everyone we serve in a one-another fashion will become a good buddy. We may be just the answer for the hour, which is fine. But we will definitely make some deeper connections in the four layers of friendship.

The outer layer is made up of acquaintances, people we know, say hello to, but rarely think about except when we happen to see them. They are people like the clerk at the grocery store, the crossing guard at the kids' school, or the pharmacist where you get your prescriptions filled.

Then there are casual friends, people we see with some regularity and with whom we have peripheral things in common. We know these folks by name. Most of us have lots of casual friends from work or the gym or church. We may sweat with these folks, worship with them, laugh with them, but we rarely cry with them.

Close friends form the third layer. We enjoy these people, seek them out. We invite them to social things with us. We discuss politics, the local sports teams, church, and spiritual issues. We know a lot about one another's histories, jobs, kids, and retirement plans. We may even vacation together. We appreciate one another and are grateful to God for one another. We aren't afraid to ask these friends to cry with us, at least up to a point.

Intimate friends are few and far between. They are the rare people who understand our hearts, who know what we are thinking. They not only laugh with us and weep with us; they also sigh with us over the deep hurts and most private of dreams. They keep our secrets as we keep theirs. They know all our foibles and flaws and choose to love us anyway.

It is the close friends and the intimate friends that we all desire. It is the lack of these friends that make us lonely. The superficial contacts of acquaintances and even casual friends will never satisfy the heart's need for closeness.

Many lonely Christians are shy folks waiting for someone at church to take an interest in them. If someone would just invite them, they'd be happy to come. They want that nudge. They need it; they long for it. They wait for it. The sad truth is that it doesn't always come.

It's not that there's a conspiracy against shy people or new people. It's that the settled folks have gotten consumed with their own agendas and daily lives. They don't mean to appear exclusive; they're just comfortable and settled. In fact, they'd be hurt if you suggested they were unkind or unwelcoming to visitors.

"So what should I do?" someone asks. "Church feels so big, so unfriendly."

I'd suggest you find a small group within the larger body. Any church, especially a large one, has many types of small groups—Sunday school classes, singles groups, couples groups, divorce recovery groups, young mothers groups, single mothers groups, empty nester groups, prayer groups, dinner groups, Bible study groups, home fellowship groups, musical groups, support groups, service groups. The list goes on and on.

The big catch in vanquishing loneliness is the risk that must be taken to do so. To attend a group for the first time can be intimidating, if not downright scary.

"What if they don't like me?"

"What if I can't think of anything to say?"

"What if I don't fit in?"

The list of fear-driven questions goes on and on. If we heed them, we remain lonely.

"We've had to move several times because of my husband's job," said Valerie. "I have found that if I want to establish a life for me and my family in a new locale, I have to take the first steps. That's hard for me because I'm not a very outgoing person. When I have to be the one to call our new church and ask when the women's Bible study meets, I know it's because no one has invited me to come with them. Every time I walk into a new group cold, knowing no one, I get clammy palms and a dry throat. But I've come to realize that it's wither or risk. I'd rather risk, even though it scares me to death every time."

A side comment Valerie made fascinated me. "Don't try to break into established friendships," she said. "Look for other new folks who are looking for friends too."

Sometimes to protect ourselves from being hurt in some as-yet-unknown but easily imagined way, we choose the loneliness we know over the risk of a painful emotional bruise. So what if dinner is Lean Cuisine eaten alone in front of the TV night after night? So what if we cry ourselves to sleep? It's safer to stay home and watch a video than to risk going to a new place with new people. In our own little fortress we are safe. We can't be hurt in a fresh way. We'll wrap ourselves in that cozy old ugly comforter of loneliness.

Or if we do decide to take the risk of trying a small group of some kind, we go in wearing more layers of emotional protection than an actress wears layers of stage makeup.

"A layer is a protective shield enabling us to quiet our fears of insecurity and insignificance while projecting a veneer of confidence."[2] We wear these layers, these masks, Crabb and Allender say, because we fear exposure. Someone will figure out that we're not perfect.

The problem is, "With layers on, we depend on our own sufficiency; with layers removed, we can trust in Him."[3]

My friend Sue used to protect herself from rejection by looking disconnected, refusing to make eye contact, and making believe she wasn't interested in what was happening around her. For years every meeting she managed to attend was an agony of protective withdrawal. Finally the loneliness drove her to begin trusting the Lord enough to remove the layers slowly, painfully, one at a time. The process took years and friends who were patient while she peeled life-long habits away.

She learned to look people in the eye. She learned that it's all right that she isn't perfect. Neither is anyone else. She learned to let her interest in what was happening show. She learned to offer her opinions. In short, she has become a different person. Now she's part of the greeting team at church, takes reservations for the women's retreat, and visits friends in a nursing home. We tease her because she has grown her fingernails for the first time in her life. They are an outward sign of the confidence she's gained in her people skills.

But developing these types of people skills and friendships brings us back to the issue of risk. We must be willing to trust God enough to take the risks necessary to overcome our loneliness.

THE COMPANIONSHIP OF GOD

The second great need we have is for connection with God. Adam and Eve walked with God in the garden, enjoying him, talking with him. When sin broke that special connection, God still sought their companionship.

"Then the man and his wife heard the sound of the LORD God as he was walking in the garden in the cool of the day, and they hid from the LORD God among the trees of the garden. But the LORD God called to the man, 'Where are you?'" (Gen. 3:8–9).

It has always been an amazing thing to me that God, the Creator of the universe, the Great I AM, the One who was and is and is to come, seeks the company of humans. Given who he is and who we are, I can only shake my head in wonder and breathe a prayer of thanks that he considers us worth wooing, worth loving, worth the death of his precious Son.

Apparently David felt the same way when he wrote,

> When I consider your heavens,
>   the work of your fingers,
> the moon and the stars,
>   which you have set in place,
> what is man that you are mindful of him,
>   the son of man that you care for him?
> O LORD, our Lord,
>   how majestic is your name in all the earth!" (Ps. 8:3–4, 9)

"I don't believe in God," Nat told me, his young face intense, as if his not believing made God's nonexistence a fact.

"That doesn't mean he's not there," I said. "It means you're choosing not to see the evidence."

And there is much evidence, starting with creation. "For since the creation of the world God's invisible qualities—his eternal power and divine nature—have been clearly seen, being understood from what has been made, so that men are without excuse" (Rom. 1:20).

Last spring for the first time migrating snow geese came to the reservoir down the road from us. I first saw them from some distance away, a great white swirl in the air, like a huge snowstorm. When I drove to the reservoir, thousands upon thousands of beautiful white geese with wings rimmed in ebony covered the water. Every so often a cluster of them would rise into the air, great wings pumping.

Always they rose in a circular movement, round and round, higher and higher, honking joyously.

We're used to the Canada geese with their white chin straps who come regularly. Often they are here in great numbers, and some remain all through the winter. But the snow geese were a special sight, a gift, a reminder of the variety and wonder of God's creative power.

And this God has sought the companionship of men and women, not because he needs us but because we need him.

David wrote of this need when he penned,

Turn to me and be gracious to me,
   for I am lonely and afflicted.
The troubles of my heart have multiplied;
   free me from my anguish.
Look upon my affliction and my distress
   and take away all my sins. (Ps. 25:16–18)

The greatest wonder of God's interest in us is that he wants to be an intimate friend, not just a casual friend or acquaintance. He wants to be our heart-friend, the One who is closer than a brother, the One who knows our secrets and bears our hurts.

Abraham is called a friend of God (James 2:23). Friend, the Greek word *philos,* is a term of endearment that refers to one who is loved. Imagine being called God's friend, being so loved by him.

The amazing thing is that we are so cherished. We are called to be his friends.

We live near the city of Philadelphia, the City of Brotherly Love, often called the City of Brotherly Shove. We are known for our impolite sports fans and our history. When William Penn first settled the area, his idea was to create a city where people loved. Human nature has prevented Penn's dream from coming true, though I'm certain there are many fine folks in Philadelphia who do care for others. Still the realities of urban life have brought Penn's dream to dust.

How about the realities of our lives? Have they brought God's desire for friendship to dust? Or have we turned our backs on our loneliness and become like Abraham, intimate with God? He already knows our thoughts and dreams, much as we might try to hide them. Why not openly share them with him and embrace his friendship rather than put up walls of protection? Why not take the risk to trust God?

Pat Johnson says that even in her sorrow over her husband's death, "Hey, I knew I wasn't alone. After all, much of my journal writing was in the form of prayers, and I knew that God was there listening to me even as I poured out my grief. As time has passed, I've learned that being alone is not that terrible. It's just the act of being left alone that's so difficult. And God never leaves us alone."

Our friend Jesse was raised in a highly dysfunctional family. Both his mother and his father were alcoholics. Jesse was the third child, unexpected and unwanted, and constantly told so.

"The anger level in our home was so high that I felt like I had to wear a bullet-proof vest to go from my bedroom to the bathroom," he says.

His father was a trucker and often away from home for days. His mother resented being alone and drank heavily during these times. She would become depressed and try to slit her wrists.

"I don't know how many times she did it," Jesse said. "At least fourteen, probably more."

His parents divorced, and his mother was so unstable that his father eventually won custody of Jesse, whom he then left with a baby-sitter as he went on his long runs. The older brothers were gone by now, leaving as quickly as they possibly could. By the time Jesse was a young man, he was drinking heavily too, to handle the emotional pain he felt daily from the constant rejection.

"I married very young, and we had a daughter," he said. "But I was too emotionally shattered to hold a marriage together, and we divorced. My goal in life became to please my buddies. I spent my money on drinks for the guys, trying to buy the acceptance I'd been denied my whole life. Alcohol became my best friend because it never rejected me."

In many ways Jesse had become his parents, but he ignored that knowledge. Even his suicidal thoughts didn't bring him up short. He could just drink them away.

One evening he was at a friend's home three doors from his own place. All those present spent the evening drinking. Eventually Jesse left for the short walk home.

"My last memory of that evening is leaving my friend's house. I don't remember the walk home or anything that followed. I woke the next morning to a trashed apartment. The refrigerator was on its side. The sofa was upended. Broken glass littered the floor. I had blood all over me. How could I have done such things and not remembered? Finally I was scared."

Jesse found a treatment program that helped him dry out. The problem was that without his best friend, alcohol, to dull his loneliness, he now had to confront it.

"I kept myself busy going to meetings and counseling sessions. When my counselor finally said that I didn't need to come any more, I was devastated. How could I spend the evening alone? To fill the time I began to counsel recovering alcoholics in worse shape than me.

"About this time I started a new job. One man sought me out and talked to me about God. He shared verses with me. I had heard enough about God in all the recovery programs to want to know more. Besides I welcomed another friend to help battle the loneliness."

Finally Jesse's new friend invited Jesse to church with him and his wife. Jesse accepted.

"He drove from his home to my home to a church where he thought I'd be happy, a round trip of at least fifty miles. He and his wife did this every Sunday for six months until they decided I was able to take myself. And I met Jesus during this time.

"God has become to me what alcohol used to be, the Friend who never deserts. I listen to tapes of men like Charles Stanley, John MacArthur, and Tony Evans. I volunteer at a local mission. I'm involved in various activities in my church. I like to keep busy. But it's God who has made all the difference."

Jesse lives alone. His daughter was killed two years ago, ironically by a drunk driver. There is no one "special" in his life. But he has found a close companionship with the Lord through his faith in Jesus, and it has changed everything. No longer does he need the bottle to champion him. He knows he's loved. His soul is satisfied.

The same possibilities for contentment are there for all who are lonely. Whether our stories are as dramatic as Jesse's or as common as mine, the same God issues the invitation to us to become his companions, close and intimate in our relationship.

"Intimacy happens when two souls rub together. It's what we long for more than anything else. To know and be known. Even in the best relationships we are still left aching for someone to comprehend our world and enter our struggle—to embrace us with a passion that seizes and melts us into a union that will never be broken. God answers that ancient longing."[4]

What a joy to be God-dependent, God-intimate, to find the lonely holes inside being filled with the rich soil of his love until we sprout with the fruit of the Spirit.

"The LORD will guide you always;
he will satisfy your needs in a sun-scorched land
and will strengthen your frame.
You will be like a well-watered garden." (Isa. 58:11)

QUESTIONS, QUESTIONS

1. Where do you have the greatest struggles with loneliness? How will you combat it?
2. Read James 2:23. How did Abraham get to be God's friend? Was this an easy process for him?
3. Read Hebrews 13:5–6. How does this help you when you are lonely and unsure?
4. Make a list of the one-another verses. How many different commands are there? What effect will they have on loneliness?
5. Solitude has been called "the needed opportunity of regaining heaven's perspective on the mysteries of life." What is the difference between *loneliness* and *solitude?*

Chapter 11

Interruptions

*If I've rested in Him quietly—and for me, only then—I have
this reservoir of strength and perspective that allows me to
regard interruptions as divine appointments.*

—Randy Alcorn

Several years ago I came home from a weeklong writer's conference full of enthusiasm and overflowing with plans. I could hardly
wait for Monday to get working on all my ideas. But first came
Easter.

We went to church and then to my in-laws for dinner. I was still
exhausted from the conference, so I came home early to take a nap.
Jeff came with me so he could take the car and go visit his girlfriend.

I had just fallen into that netherworld of half sleep when the
front door flew open and crashed against the wall. I could hear Jeff

panting, saying over and over, "I can't believe I did it. I can't believe I did it."

I pulled myself from bed and staggered down the hall to him.

"What did you do?" I asked, uncertain what I was going to hear but knowing I wouldn't like it.

He had driven off the road in front of Mr. Spotts's house. Mr. Spotts lived about a quarter of a mile away down the street and around the corner.

"See, a piece of film negative was resting on the dash," Jeff explained. "I had the windows open because it's such a warm day. When I turned the corner by Mr. Spotts's place, the wind caught the film and started to blow it toward the far window. I grabbed it before it could get out the window. Then to keep it safe, I put it on the floor."

The trouble was that when he leaned over to put the film down, he, like many new drivers, brought the wheel with him. When he straightened up, he was off the road, heading for a huge maple tree. He hit the brakes, missed the tree, but took out the Escort's undercarriage on a huge rock.

Jeff and I walked outside and looked down the street. We live in a semirural area, and Mr. Spotts's house was visible across an open field. I could see Mr. Spotts himself walking around our damaged car.

To grasp the nuances of the situation, you must understand that nine months prior our older son Chip had had an accident in front of Mr. Spotts's house too. Chip had been driving to his summer job in the Chevette. He came to the corner by Mr. Spotts's, slowed and turned. To his surprise a backhoe was chugging down the street in front of him, lights blinking warnings about its slow speed.

Chip pulled out to pass the backhoe just as it turned left toward a small dirt road. The backhoe picked Chip up and deposited him and the car in Mr. Spotts's giant hedge. When the insurance company handed out checks, the Chevette was valued at $4,000. The hedge was valued at $7,000.

So when Jeff and I reached Mr. Spotts, he was quite familiar with our family. He looked at me and simply said, "Mrs. Roper."

I looked solemnly back and said, "Mr. Spotts."

He turned his gaze to Jeff. "Is this the same one?"

I shook my head. "No. This is his brother. But," I hurried to assure him, "we have no more."

The upshot was that we needed another car. The Escort that had replaced the Chevette now had to be replaced, but this time we decided to go with a big, old car that had lots of heavy metal in its body.

"Look," said Chuck, rubbing at the headache he had developed, "I've got to go to work all week. The boys have got to go to school. Gayle, you're the only one with lots of time. You can look for a car."

"What?" My usual job when we buy a car is to pick the color, and I like it that way.

"And Jeff can pay for it with his summer job."

All three of the males left the room, satisfied. Well, I wouldn't say Jeff was exactly satisfied as he foresaw a long, poor summer ahead, but he understood. I, on the other hand, sat there and stewed.

Wait a minute! I thought. *Even if I knew what I was doing, I don't have the time. I've got plans! I've got ideas I want to explore. I've got books and articles to write.*

Interruptions. They *always* seem to come at the most inopportune, inconvenient moments. I've often wondered why that is. After all, we worship a God of order and planning.

We see his order in the precise steps of creation. We talk frequently about the plan of salvation. Christ talked about it not yet being his time to suffer, until, of course, he said, "My time has come." And his hour was perfect for us because, "You see, at just the right time, when we were still powerless, Christ died for the ungodly" (Rom. 5:6). There's also a time set for Christ's return, though only God the Father knows when that is. Divine order. Structure.

Scripture further reveals God's planning through the pattern in the tapestry of Israel's history. Never did God forget that nation. In fact he said to them, "For I know the plans I have for you, . . . plans to prosper you and not to harm you, plans to give you hope and a future" (Jer. 29:11).

So why are our lives so full of interruptions that knock our plans awry? Some days it's like life is one great potholed road, and we fall into every pothole out there.

One answer is that God is not only a God of order, but he is also a God of the long view. He wants to accomplish certain things both in history and in us as individuals, and sometimes interruptions are the best ways to do it. He foresees the end result of all the glitches when often all we see is the present chaos and frustration.

One example of what I mean is reflected in the verse quoted above where God talks about the wonderful plans he has for Israel. He speaks of his plans to bless the nation while it is in the middle of seventy years in Babylonian bondage. Seventy years! With thousands carried off into captivity. Talk about an interruption!

But God still had a plan, just as he does through our interruptions, unwelcome as they may be.

We're going to define an *interruption* as "anything that disturbs what we perceive to be our life patterns." Frequently these disturbances are merely frustrating, like my having to put aside my writing plans for a few days when we needed a new car. At most these *petty interruptions* are mere blips on the radar screen of life, not worth the agitation they often foment in us.

When Chuck and I were dating, he would drive down every weekend from Bethlehem, Pennsylvania, where he was in graduate school at Lehigh University, to my parents' home in Audubon, New Jersey, where I lived my first year out of college. We got engaged in December of that year.

My grandmother lived with my family at that time, and she was convinced that Chuck and I had too much time alone for "spooning." She went to my mother and expressed her concerns.

"Mother," my mom said, "the kids only see each other on weekends. They have very little time together. They're getting married in a few months. They need this time alone."

Grandmom continued to disagree. She decided that if my parents weren't going to protect my virtue, she would.

My parents' home was laid out with a sunporch on the far right, then moving to the left, the living room, a central hall, and the dining room. Attached to the house was a suite of rooms off the dining room, rooms that had once housed a doctor's practice. These rooms were now my grandmother's rooms.

One night Chuck and I were sitting in the sunroom cuddling. That's Christian cuddling, which, like Christian romances, is chaste but promising. Suddenly I got that feeling of being stared at. You know what I mean—the itchy sensation in the center of your back. I looked across the darkened living room, across the darkened hall, and into the darkened dining room, and there stood Grandmom in her nightgown, staring at Chuck and me. She proceeded to take up that position for the next several weekends.

It was an interruption, to be sure, in spite of the fact that Grandmom could barely see five feet in front of her in bright sunlight. I have no idea what she thought she saw those weeks of being the watchman on the wall, but I can imagine. Finally she seemed to get tired of standing in the cold and gave up her sentry's responsibility.

Lots of interruptions are like this one—frustrating, bothersome, but not earthshaking.

There's the kid who throws up just as you're about to leave for an evening out.

There's the parent/chauffeur who is needed just as it's time to sit down for dinner.

There's the milk that the careless child spills, and which drips all over your new slacks.

There's the broken washing machine that always seems to stop working with a tub full of hot, soapy water.

There's the missing sock that said washing machine ate.

There's the missing shoe when you know the child had a matched pair yesterday.

Bothersome, petty, not earth-shattering.

Sometimes, though, interruptions are *very upsetting.* They put a major crimp in our plans and a monkey in our wrench.

The pastor suddenly resigns, and the church is left shepherdless.

The company reorganizes, and our job is drastically changed.

The roof needs replacing at the same time the college tuition bill arrives, both on the heels of a huge repair bill on the car.

Very upsetting.

Several years ago Christian Herald Books released a Holocaust biography I'd written with a Messianic Jewish woman of Hungarian descent named Marianne Fischer. *Time of Storm* told a great story of

God's care in terrible situations, and Marianne was rightfully excited about her book.

Two weeks after *Time of Storm* was released, Christian Herald went out of the book business. All the salesmen were fired, and the books were all warehoused. Distribution was limited to what Marianne and I could manage through our speaking. A dream of many years standing was lost to Marianne, and months of hard work were lost to me.

Serious disappointment.

And then there are the *life-altering interruptions,* the things that happen that prevent life from ever being what we expected or hoped for.

Late-in-life babies when we thought we finally were going to be free to pursue some personal plans.

Illnesses that lay us low for a length of time or that take the life of someone we know and love.

Job losses or transfers that alter the whole rhythm of our lives and force changes on us that we had never foreseen.

Divorces that cause us to rewrite our future.

Death that robs us of the comfort and companionship of someone we had hoped to enjoy for years.

Rebellious children who drain us and turn our homes into armed camps.

Sometimes we understand why these interruptions, big or small, come because God in his grace gives us a glimpse of his plans. Such is the situation with my sterility.

Because I couldn't have children, we adopted. Because of our adoption, Chip and Jeff were raised in a Christian home with a strong, godly father. When Chip finally met his birth mother a few years ago, she told him that one of the reasons she released him was because she wanted him to have a father who loved him and wanted him. Chip was able to assure her that he got exactly what she had desired.

But many times the reasons for interruptions aren't always so clear.

My nephew Chad decided to give the summer between his junior and senior years in college to missions. He studied his options carefully and prayerfully. He finally decided on a mission that dealt with ecological issues as well as ministry, thinking that such a work would be able to make use of his engineering training.

He applied and was accepted by the mission board, got his shots, bought his tickets, and, shortly after school ended that spring, winged his way to South America. He got off the plane, and to his consternation, no one was there to meet him. He waited and waited until finally a man pulled up.

"I'm not the person you'll be working with," he said. "I'll take you to him."

Chad climbed into the Jeep and away they went into the jungle. Eventually they reached a primitive building site.

"This is it," the driver said.

Chad climbed out, not a happy camper, because there was no one there except an eighteen-year-old who'd also come for summer missions.

"Don't worry," the driver said. "He'll be here soon." And he left.

The missionary in charge never came. Chad and his companion survived on canned tuna. Finally after two weeks the driver returned to make certain the boys were all right.

"I'm going home," said Chad. "I didn't come here to sit in the jungle with nothing to do. I came here to work, but if no one cares enough to oversee me, I want to leave."

Several pounds lighter and wondering what had gone wrong, Chad returned home. Soon he got a phone call from the president of the mission, all apologies and profound regret. Somehow Chad's project, Chad himself, and the boy at the jungle site had fallen through the cracks.

But Chad is left with questions. Why, when he did everything right, did it all go wrong? How did it go wrong? Who was supposed to be there and wasn't? Why wasn't he? Has this ever happened before? What if he or the other boy had been injured or taken sick during that time alone?

No answers.

How are we supposed to deal with these interruptions when we have carefully, prayerfully laid plans that go wrong? How should we handle the obstructions to our schemes, adventures, and ideas?

Let me tell you another story to set up my answer.

I have always loved hats. I wore them until it was so unstylish that I finally gave up. But I kept my favorites just in case hats ever became popular again.

Finally I had to admit that even if hats came back into vogue, my hats would no longer make the cut. They were just too dated. I gave them to my oldest granddaughter Ashley to play with when she was about seven.

"These hats were my favorites," I told her. "But this one." I took a black felt Australian-styled hat with one brim turned up and put it on. "This hat was my favorite."

I smiled happily at Ashley.

She looked at me quite seriously. "Grandmom," she asked kindly, "did people laugh at you when you wore it?"

I blinked, took the hat off, and smiled. "No, sweetie, at least not that I ever heard."

Looking unconvinced, she took the hats and put them on the shelf in the kids' closet in the basement. They still sit there, gathering dust.

I've thought about Ashley's comments quite a bit. Why did the hat look so silly to her and yet was a favorite of mine? I've decided that more is involved than changing styles and generational fashion sense. I've decided it has to do with memories.

That black hat meant nothing to Ashley because she had no point of reference for it, but to me it was special. I bought it to wear when Millersville University in Millersville, Pennsylvania, named the new dining hall Gordinier Hall after my grandfather, Dr. Charles H. Gordinier, who had once been president of the school. I see the hat, and I think of Grandpop.

I think of the slight man who washed his birdbath out every night and who played a mean game of croquet. I think of the man who at forty-two married a twenty-year-old who had been one of his students and who lived long enough to celebrate his fiftieth wedding anniversary. I think of the man who went bald by thirty, who was in the Oklahoma Land Rush, and who gave us silver dollars every year for Christmas. I think of the man who smoked smelly cigars and who had an asthmatic cough that scared me to death as a child. I thought it would certainly kill him. I think of the man who worked until he was ninety-two years old and who died at ninety-five one week after a stroke, his only illness.

Memories are the secret to that hat—and to dealing with our interruptions.

"Has God forgotten to be merciful?
    Has he in anger withheld his compassion?" *Selah*
Then I thought, "To this I will appeal:
    the years of the right hand of the Most High."
I will remember the deeds of the LORD;
    yes, I will remember your miracles of long ago.

I will meditate on all your works
    and consider all your mighty deeds.
Your ways, O God, are holy.
    What god is so great as our God?
Your path led through the sea,
        your way through the mighty waters,
        though your footprints were not seen. (Ps. 77:9–13, 19)

Sometimes when interruptions stir our lives with all the ruthless-ness of a blender on high speed, and we feel like tomato puree, all pulverized and reeling, we need to remember what the psalmist said. "To this I will appeal: the years of the right hand of the Most High. I will remember . . ."

First, the psalmist says, he will remember *the deeds of the Lord.*

When the psalmist talked about the deeds of the Lord, he was talking about the written history of God working on behalf of his nation, Israel.

God preserved Noah and his family in the flood.

God gave Abraham and Sarah a son in their old age.

God provided a lamb for Abraham to sacrifice instead of his son, Isaac.

God kept Joseph safe in spite of his brothers' intentions.

God brought Israel, several million strong, out of Egypt under Moses.

God protected Israel in the wilderness.

God led Israel into the Promised Land under Joshua.

Today we can recall many more examples of God's care, more recent occurrences that the psalmist knew nothing of, more recent being relative.

God kept Shadrach, Meshach, and Abednego safe in the fiery furnace and Daniel in the lion's den.

God brought his people out of Babylonian captivity and back to the land.

God called a maid named Mary to bear a Child.

God raised his Son from the dead on the third day.

God established his church.

What mighty deeds indeed. They are our proof that, despite appearances, despite interruptions, God has a plan. God is in control.

And our memories need not be limited only to the works of our Lord recorded in his Word. How about all the memories we have of God working in our lives as he writes our personal Christian histories.

Obviously the longer we're Christians, the more complex our personal Christian histories become, but even a new believer has the memory of his salvation story.

I love salvation stories because they're never the same. God works individually to bring us to himself, setting into play circumstances and relationships that culminate in our confession of Christ as Lord. One of the first memories in my personal Christian history is Margie from down the street and her invitation to Sunday school.

Another memory that means much to me is from the days in ninth grade. As I mentioned, I had a wonderful family, but I longed for someone who was praying for me. All my other friends at church seemed to have parents who prayed for them. I missed that special evidence of care.

One Sunday Mrs. Abel saw me as I was getting ready to go up the steps to the balcony where we girls usually sat during church.

"Gayle," she called and limped over to me. She was a polio survivor and the mother of one of the guys a year younger than I. "I just wanted to tell you that I pray for you every day." She smiled, turned, and walked away. I smiled, turned, and walked upstairs, hugging her comment to my heart. God knew my yearning, and he provided an answer for something I hadn't even dared pray for.

Another personal memory developed many years later. We were married, living in Chuck's hometown, and had both boys. After a hurtful church experience, Chuck and I became involved in a fellowship group that met in homes. We met together each Sunday for a year, and our brother-in-law Ken, who had just returned from serving in the chaplaincy in Vietnam, preached for us each week. At the end of the year, however, we knew we were just playing church. Ken was finishing his year of graduate work and moving on; we as a group had had a wonderful time of healing our hurts, building friendships, and sharing; but a church was meant to be more than we were. It was time to disband and find homes in local congregations.

We gathered for our final service at our home. We enjoyed a meal together. Everyone was about to leave when the phone rang. It was the mother of one of the men in our group of seventeen.

"I know this is your final day of meeting, but I thought you might like to know that they announced in our church this morning that we're having a speaker on Wednesday night. His job is to go around establishing new churches. Maybe you'd like to hear him before you abandon all."

Instead of dispersing forever, we sent four people to hear this gentleman whose name I have long forgotten. He then met with our small group. Today our congregation averages about two thousand on a Sunday morning, and we refer to that strategic phone call as the phone call from heaven.

The deeds of the Lord.

"Your ways, O God, are holy. What god is so great as our God?" (Ps. 77:13).

Asaph, the psalmist, reminds us that we can deal with life's difficulties because of the God we worship. We remember not only what
he has done but also *the very character of God himself.*

It is who God is that makes remembering him valuable. His
attributes, his intrinsic self, make resting in him possible when all
around is chaotic.

"What is God?" asks the Westminster Shorter Catechism. "God
is a Spirit, infinite, eternal, and unchangeable in His being, wisdom,
power, holiness, justice, goodness, and truth."

How can we possibly get our minds around a God who is all
these things? How can we ever understand him? He is so far above
us that even the cleverest of people can grasp but a soupçon of his
breadth and depth and height and width.

So to try to comprehend him, we take him apart. We talk about
his various attributes as if we can actually separate them one from the
other. Of course we can't, but until we can devise a better way to
grasp the ungraspable, we will continue to examine him piece by
piece. We speak of his love as if it were a separate thing from his justice. Or maybe we're discussing his grace or his mercy or, if we're very
brave, his wrath.

My less-than-satisfactory way of viewing God is to compare
him to a string of pearls. Each pearl is like an attribute or characteristic of God. Each pearl with its luminescent sheen and lustrous
beauty is very valuable by itself, a thing to be appreciated and
enjoyed. But it is the whole of the string of pearls that has the real
value because the pearls balance one another and enhance one
another.

So it's the whole of God that we must never forget, where each
characteristic or attribute balances another. His love balances his
justice, which balances his grace, which balances his wrath, which

balances his mercy, which balances his wisdom, which balances his omnipotence, which balances . . .

"Our aim in studying the Godhead must be to know God Himself better."[1] One of the best lessons about God is from God himself in his conversation with Job, a man who suffered many major interruptions in his life when he lost his children, his servants, his crops—everything but his wife, and she cursed him and God. Rather than sympathize with Job, God reminds him who has the authority and power, who has allowed the obstacles to Job's plan for life.

> "Have you ever given orders to the morning,
>   or shown the dawn its place?
> What is the way to the abode of light?
>   And where does darkness reside?
> Can you take them to their places?
>   Do you know the paths to their dwellings?
> Have you entered the storehouses of the snow
>   or seen the storehouses of the hail,
> which I reserve for times of trouble,
>   for days of war and battle?" (Job 38:12, 19–20, 22–23)

God continues, reminding Job over and over who he is.

> "What is the way to the place where the lightning is dispersed,
>   or the place where the east winds are scattered over the
>   earth?
> Who cuts a channel for the torrents of rain,
>   and a path for the thunderstorm,
> to water a land where no man lives,

a desert with no one in it,
to satisfy a desolate wasteland
and make it sprout with grass?" (v. 24–27)

Surely by this time, Job is reeling, just as we should be in light of who God is. For all our human wisdom, we know next to nothing.

"Can you bind the beautiful Pleiades?
Can you loose the cords of Orion?
Can you bring forth the constellations in their seasons
or lead out the Bear with its cubs?
Do you know the laws of the heavens?
Can you set up God's dominion over the earth?
Can you raise your voice to the clouds
and cover yourself with a flood of water?
Do you send the lightning bolts on their way?
Do they report to you, 'Here we are'?
Who endowed the heart with wisdom
or gave understanding to the mind?
Who has the wisdom to count the clouds?
Who can tip over the water jars of the heavens
when the dust becomes hard
and the clods of earth stick together?" (vv. 31–38)
Only you, Lord. Only you.

Then Job answered the LORD:
"I am unworthy—how can I reply to you?
I put my hand over my mouth." (40:3–4)

God is most definitely power and authority, but he is also personable. The Westminster Shorter Catechism states that the chief end of man is "to love God and enjoy him forever." Learning to enjoy God, to laugh with him, trust him, is not an academic exercise like trying to get our minds around his greatness can become. Enjoying God means taking that string of pearls and wearing the entire rope. It means learning to be content because he and what he provides are enough.

"I am *overcome with joy* because of your unfailing love," writes David, "for you have seen my troubles, and you care about the anguish of my soul. You have not handed me over to my enemy but have set me in a safe place" (Ps. 31:8–9 NLT, italics mine).

The trouble is that sometimes we and God define "a safe place" differently.

My friend Shirley taught junior-high girls in Sunday school for years. One year she had a particularly recalcitrant group who had no interest in learning. Somehow Shirley discovered that the girls liked to sing, so they sang for quite a while every Sunday.

"I made certain that every week we sang 'God Is So Good.' I was determined that they would get one piece of doctrine whether they recognized it as such or not."

Near the end of that year, Shirley found herself sitting in the doctor's office learning that she had breast cancer.

"As I sat there on the table, I realized that 'God Is So Good' wasn't for my Sunday school girls. It was for me. Breast cancer or not, God is still good."

Shirley recognized that even breast cancer, along with all the interruptions inherent in its presence, was a safe place when she was there with God—because God is who he is.

QUESTIONS, QUESTIONS

1. Think about the life of Joseph. How many major interruptions can you recall? Read Genesis 50:20. How did Joseph perceive the interruptions?

2. Read Romans 11:33–36. What in this doxology makes it easier for you to trust in the time of interruptions?

3. Read Psalm 119:55. Why is it so important to remember God in the night?

4. Read Psalm 119:52. Where does the psalmist find comfort? Why?

5. Read Psalm 105:5–10. Who does the remembering? What comfort is found in remembering?

Chapter 12

Divine Discontent

Some discontent is sheer whining. But not all is a wrong spirit.
God sometimes makes us uncomfortable to pry us out of our ruts.
—Charles D. Kelley

Now that we've spent hours talking about finding contentment, I want to suggest that there is a thing called divine discontent. It's a restless feeling, a disquiet. Something's not quite right, but we're not certain what. It eats at us, pulls at us, even upsets us.

Divine discontent is God's gentle—or not so gentle—nudge leading us in a new direction. He has a new job for us, a new ministry, a change of some kind. Even though we rest content in him and obey him and love him, there is still this unease. It makes us nervous. It might even make us doubt the truth of our resting in him.

Charles D. Kelley writes, "Dreaming often begins with a nudge, a discontent with what is, a dissatisfaction with a relationship, an uneasiness with offered solutions."[1]

There's a lot of truth in Kelley's words. The dreamer, the curious, and the creative are never satisfied with their talents and their uses. The explorer is always looking for new things to explore. The adventurer wants a new adventure. The inventor hungers for new discoveries.

This restlessness is the kind that tells you that you can do better next time. You can write a better book, sing a better concert, build a better mousetrap, invent a better contraption. You can discover the answer to that scientific unknown or solve that mathematical problem. This inner urging for more is what has led us to all the discoveries of the ages. It led Marco Polo to China, Columbus to America, and the astronauts to the moon. It will lead men and women to unlock countless more of the mysteries of the universe. It led me to write this book and you to read it.

But a holy dissatisfaction is different. Divine discontent is experienced by God's people when he wants to initiate change in their lives. Nehemiah is a good example of one who experienced this godly nudging.

He was in exile with the Jews during the seventy years in Babylon and developed a great burden for those who had returned to Jerusalem to reestablish the land. When he heard about the trouble and disgrace back home, he said, "I sat down and wept. For some days I mourned and fasted and prayed before the God of heaven" (Neh. 1:4).

Nehemiah was the king's cupbearer and was in the king's presence often.

"I had not been sad in his presence before, so the king asked me, 'Why does your face look so sad when you are not ill? It can be nothing but sadness of heart'" (Neh. 2:2).

Nehemiah explained his sorrow over Judah and asked for permission to return to build the gates and walls of Jerusalem. The king allowed him to return, and the project of restoring God's testimony once again moved forward.

But it all began with a restlessness, a divine discontent in Nehemiah's heart.

When God sends such feelings to us, we need to heed them. We need to pray as Nehemiah did, seeking God's reasons for these feelings. "For some days I mourned and fasted and prayed before the God of heaven." And we need to remember that the reasons for this inner squirming are as varied as the people who experience the feeling.

Perhaps God wants to move us from our present circumstances.

My friend Linda Ingham had served for years as founder and director of REST Ministries here in our town, a work that deals with women in need, frequently women in prison. The work grew and became established under Linda's leadership. Through Bible studies and counseling, a highly competent staff worked with women while they were in prison and after they were released. REST established seminars to train others to work with hurting women from victims of abuse to victims of divorce, opened a secondhand shop to provide work for women coming out of prison, and developed written material to expand its scope.

Then a divine discontent seized Linda. She sought the Lord to understand why. She realized that for her, part of the joy is in establishing a work. Once it's thriving, the challenge has gone, and she is content to let someone else carry it on.

After several months of prayer, Linda resigned from REST and moved to another area to begin the Jesus Connection of Lancaster County, Pennsylvania, another ministry to hurting women in an area where none previously existed. She moved in answer to divine discontent.

However, novelist Athol Dickson found his experience with divine discontent completely different in outcome.

"There was a time in my life," writes Athol, "when I felt so dissatisfied with my career as an architect that I literally fell to my knees in tears of frustration. Going to work each day was a depressing thing to do, even though I owned the company. For months I asked God to let me change the way I spent my time. I got more and more desperate.

"Finally I received a clear answer. It was: 'No. Stay where you are.'

"Nothing had changed in my situation, but God's answer was undeniable. I knew it was wrong to continue feeling discontented. My prayer changed from 'Get me out of here' to 'Show me why I'm here.' That was all it took for contentment to settle back in. When I quit looking for contentment 'out there,' and accepted that God wanted me right where I was, he began to show me possibilities and opportunities in my situation that I had overlooked before. My firm took on new life, doubled in size, and eventually became successful enough to allow me to partially retire at the age of forty-two.

"Is it possible that 'divine discontent' is sometimes given to lead us to a greater obedience to God, right where we are?"

Yet another reason for holy restlessness could be that we need to learn some truth, spiritual or secular.

Rosene was a registered nurse for several years when she decided to go for a Bachelor of Science in Nursing. It was a struggle with her job, her family, and the requirements of her courses, but she loved the academic atmosphere and challenge. She flourished.

"Then suddenly I didn't want to go to classes any more. My enthusiasm was completely gone, and I still had half the program to complete with the dream of continuing for my master's. I couldn't understand what was happening."

After praying about what to do, Rosene contacted her college.

"Just how much class work do I still have to complete?" she asked.

"Just let me pull your records," her advisor said. Then, "Hmm."

Oh, no, Rosene thought. *It's worse than I feared.*

"You know we've become more flexible in our policy since you enrolled?"

"No, I didn't know. What's the bad news?"

"No bad news. Good news. We have decided to accept all your course credits from nursing school. We don't usually do that, but you were a 4.0 student, and your work here has been exemplary. You only have one class left to take to get your degree."

Rosene's eyes shone as she recounted the story. "If I hadn't felt discontent, I'd never have checked on my remaining classes. I would have assumed I needed several more just like I'd been told when I enrolled. But the Lord saved me all that duplication of effort, all that time, and all that money. Now I can't wait to get that last class under my belt."

When we feel a holy uneasiness, a restlessness, we need to do as Nehemiah did, as Linda, Athol, and Rosene did. We need to go to the Lord and plead with him to teach us what he wants us to know. We then need to act, either moving on as Nehemiah and Linda did, staying where we are in obedience and with a godly attitude as Athol did, or checking our options as Rosene did. The one thing we must not do is whine. Divine discontent demands of us the very same thing contentment does: obedience to God's call on our lives.

QUESTIONS, QUESTIONS

1. Read Psalm 32:8. What is the promise for times of divine discontent? Have you ever experienced divine discontent? How did you face it? What was the outcome?

2. Read Romans 8:26–27. What comfort is there here for us in times of confusion and divine discontent?

3. Read Romans 8:28. If "works all things for good" means "conforms us to Christ," what do you learn about divine discontent?

4. Read Romans 8:31–32. What do these verses teach us of God's heart for us whether we are struggling in times of divine discontent or are sailing along in contentment?

5. Read Romans 8:37–38. When you feel confused by your divine discontent, what are the promises of Scripture?

Chapter 13

Obedience

All true knowledge of God is born out of obedience.
—John Calvin

I grew up with two younger brothers who, like most boy children, had a limitless taste for wrestling and roughhousing. It cost them many a bruise, many a scrape, many a tear to indulge. It even cost my younger brother a front tooth. But nothing ever deterred them for long.

One of their favorite places to wrestle was their bedroom, where they seemed to assume "out of sight, out of mind"—like our parents couldn't tell what was going on when the ceiling shook, and thuds, muffled groans, and grunts drifted down the stairwell.

Mom would go to the bottom of the stairs and call, "Are you boys wrestling up there? You know I don't like you wrestling. You'll hurt yourselves or the furniture."

A sudden silence veiled the house, followed by whispers and a quiet scramble from above. Then an innocent voice, usually belonging to the elder of the two, would float down. "No, Mom. We're not wrestling. We're just sitting here on the beds talking."

My mother would look at me with a like-I-believe-that roll of her eyes, but she didn't press the issue. She'd gotten what she wanted, peace and quiet, at least for the moment.

We often look at obedience like my brothers used to. The rules are there, known and understood. If we get caught breaking the rules, we suddenly scramble to do what's right to save face or to avoid punishment. Otherwise we wrestle whenever and wherever we want.

But that's not obedience. That's responding to an authority greater than we are because there's not really much choice. It's do what they ask or suffer the consequences of disobeying.

Godly obedience, on the other hand, is compliance with respect and deference. Godly obedience is voluntary, a gift we offer to the Father we love. As an English gentleman uses a butter knife even when dining alone, so an obedient Christian does what God asks even when there's no one to be impressed.

There are many specifics in Scripture for us to obey. Love one another. Have nothing to do with the works of darkness. Go into the world and preach the gospel. Trust in the Lord with all your heart. Rejoice in the Lord always. Draw near to God with a sincere heart. Put off old patterns and put on new ones. Speak the truth in love. Love the Lord your God with all your heart, mind, and spirit.

And nothing shows better that we have this overwhelming love for God in our hearts, minds, and spirits than our willing obedience. We comply with his standards by choice, and through our obedience we find contentment, satisfaction, rest.

"And this is love: that we walk in obedience to his commands. As you have heard from the beginning, his command is that you walk in love" (2 John 6).

I love the circular logic of John's thoughts on love and obedience. If you love the Lord, you obey him. And his command for you to obey is that you love. And if you love him, you obey him. And his command for you to obey is to love.

"To me," says novelist Athol Dickson, "Christian contentment is a manifestation of obedience. Since Jesus said loving the One God and loving others is the pinnacle of obedience (Mark 12:28–43), it seems to me contentedness begins with love. Agape love is a reflection of the Source of all love, so drawing nearer to him through increasing commitment to obedience is revealed in greater love within ourselves for God, our neighbor, and ourselves."

Following the Lord in obedience and her husband to seminary, my friend Lucy McGuire remembers, "During the lean years my husband was in seminary, I struggled to find contentment with less. Not only did I avoid buying anything; I didn't even go window shopping. Gradually I began to be at peace with very little.

"When my mother came to visit for the first time, I tried to explain my new contentment. 'I would be happy anywhere as long as I have God—even if we lived in the slums.'

"She looked out the window, then back at me with pity. 'Honey, this is the slums.'

"But I was as happy there as I'd been previously living in a seven-bedroom house on several acres. My joy did not and does not depend on whether I have a certain amount. It rests on my relationship with God. He is enough."

Lucy says it well. God and what he provides are enough. Obeying him, loving him, and trusting his provision throw open the doorway through which we enter the corridors of contentment. It's really quite simple, at least in theory.

But what about obeying God when we can't see where he's leading us? Granted, there's always an unknown quality about the future, but sometimes God asks us to walk completely blind.

Imagine the Hebrew multitude on the shores of the Red Sea. The Egyptians are chasing them, bearing down, furious, and loaded for bear. Ahead is a great expanse of water. No escape. The Israelites are terrified and cry to the Lord. Later, they grumble to Moses, saying, "It would have been better for us to serve the Egyptians than to die in the desert!" (Exod. 14:12).

"The Lord will fight for you; you need only to be still" Moses replies (14:14).

Then Moses stretches forth his staff and a great wind blows, the waters part, damming up in great liquid walls on either side. The wind dries the floor of the sea, and the Israelites step forth in obedience and faith.

This scene is forever colored for me by the movie *The Ten Commandments*. Moses is Charlton Heston standing on the rock stretching forth his arm. The Israelites are forever the quiet, scared, awe-struck people walking between the walls of water.

I don't think that depiction of the people is that erroneous. I try to picture myself walking between those walls of water, obeying but terrified that something will give way and the water will crash down on me at any minute. Would I be eye to eye with a fish or a crocodile, safe in its water world on the other side of the wall? What if I touched the wall? Would it spring a leak? As a slave, I've lived in a land of multiple gods for many, many years, and those gods are fickle and often cruel. What about the One God that Moses calls us back to? Would he play a cruel practical joke on us and send us all to a watery grave?

Obedience

"Your path led through the sea, / your way through the mighty waters, / though your footprints were not seen" (Ps. 77:19).

How many times does God ask us to step forward where there are no footprints? No clearly articulated plan? No foreseen conclusion? "The very nature of the obedience he demands is that it be given without regard to circumstances or results."[1]

But for some of us, obedience seems too simple or too unexciting or too passive. We don't see the challenge of obedience for what it is: the supernatural development of courage and strength to stand against the flow of culture in a world wracked with sin. We prefer instead life as an extended chess game, and with careful plotting and planning we try to control the outcome of things.

If I do this, then she'll do that.

If I say this, then he'll say that. Then I'll say this, he'll say that, and I'll move in for the kill.

Such machinations aren't obedience but manipulation. There is no trusting God here, but strategy and selfish goals.

Rebekah fell into the trap of playing chess with her twin sons' lives. When Esau, the older brother, was preparing to receive his father's blessing, Rebekah finagled circumstances so that Jacob was blessed instead (see Gen. 27). We can't begin to appreciate what a momentous thing the blessing was in that culture, for we have nothing comparable. We can, however, appreciate its importance as we see the overwhelming damage done by Rebekah's manipulations.

"Pretend you're your brother," she told Jacob.

"But I don't look like him. He's hairy and I'm not."

"So disguise yourself with goat pelts. Your father's vision is bad. He'll never know. And I'll make Isaac's favorite stew just like Esau does. You can take it to him and get the blessing."

Jacob does deceive Isaac and receive the blessing, but at great cost to everyone. Jacob must flee to escape from his older brother's wrath at being tricked and robbed, and he's gone from his family and homeland for twenty years. Rebekah loses her favorite son when he flees, and she never sees him again. I assume she lost Esau's affection when he realized what she had done to him, and she certainly must have put a big strain on her marriage when Isaac realized she masterminded the deception.

The fascinating thing about this story is that the promise from God had always been that Esau, the elder, would serve Jacob, the younger (Gen. 25:23), the very thing Rebekah finagled to achieve. However, none of the characters were content to wait for God to work. All were plotting and planning—Esau to get a blessing he felt was his but that God said wasn't, Rebekah to circumvent God's plan for Jacob to rule with her own corrupt plan for the very same thing, and Jacob to step in without considering right and wrong, greedily grabbing the opportunity. Even the duped Isaac planned to bless the elder against God's wishes.

All lost and learned that contentment does not lie in managing and manipulating. It lies rather in obedience and following God through the great adventure that is life, saying, "Amen. Amen. I agree. God will provide what I need when I need it."

"I have found," writes novelist Lyn Cote, "the secret of contentment for me is never presuming to predict the outcome of any adventure in which I am involved. That way, no matter what I get, I'm pleased and surprised."

Too bad Rebekah didn't understand this concept of letting God do as he will, of trusting the Lord to accomplish his purposes in his time. She remains forever a warning against taking things into our own hands no matter what our motive.

In total contrast to Rebekah stands Paul, who writes, "Follow my example, as I follow the example of Christ" (1 Cor. 11:1). Only a man living a life of obedience would dare say something like this. Only women who long after God, who yearn for contentment and are willing to be obedient, will accept the challenge of living in such a fashion themselves that others may use them as models. But oh the impact of these women who so live!

"I saw contentment in my great-grandmother, my grandmother, and I continue to see it in my mother," writes novelist Deborah Raney. "Not all my siblings 'inherited' the tendency to contentment like I did, but I do think some of the reason I 'got' it is because I saw it beautifully modeled by three generations before me."

Being obedient, of course, doesn't mean that life will always be full of all good things. The young Shadrach, Meshach, and Abednego obeyed and ended up in a furnace. Granted they survived, but they didn't know that going in, and history is full of stories of those who didn't. Daniel as an old man of ninety ended up in the lion's den because he obeyed. Although he too survived, he didn't know that he would when they led him away. And again we must never forget the many through history for whom the lions' mouths were not closed. Obedience may come with a steep price tag.

But the object of obedience is not to survive at any cost but to willingly submit ourselves to the will of God. The mature Christian "knows that he can afford to die now that he is in Christ, but he knows that he cannot afford to do wrong, and this knowledge becomes a gyroscope to stabilize his thinking and his acting."[2]

Another interesting concept comes into play in stabilizing us. It's the principle that as we desire more and more to be obedient, this requires that we learn more and more of Christ. As a result, we will find that we receive more and more of the things that matter to us. It's just like David said: "Delight yourself in the LORD and he will give you the desires of your heart" (Ps. 37:4).

It's not that God caves in and gives us all that we ask for. It's that our hearts are turned, and that what's important to him becomes important to us. In fact, we don't even want the things we used to want. We now know they aren't important. "A believer who has learned the skill of contentment has been enabled by God to be satisfied even in the worst conditions. At the same time, however, he can never again be satisfied with the shallow substitutes for contentment that the world has (to offer)."[3]

They came, some two thousand strong, from all over the Congo, national pastors intent on attending the rare and wonderful conference being held just for them. Literally risking their lives, they traveled through their war-torn country to hear the Word of God taught. One typical group traveled two days by foot, six days by canoe, and went through seventeen military checkpoints. At each checkpoint their lives were at risk, and any monies or food they managed to obtain were confiscated. Another group, a small choir, traveled five days by foot for the joy of singing one song for the assembled pastors and their honored Western guests.

One of our pastors, Carl Green, was privileged to be one of the guests and speakers at this conference. He was returning to the country where he was born to missionary parents some forty years before.[4]

"I was frequently moved to tears by the commitment of these believers and the depth of their hearts for God in the face of extraordinarily difficult circumstances," Carl told us, his eyes becoming glassy with tears. "I knew that in six months some of these leaders would be dead of malnutrition. Others would be forced to face death at the hands of the Ugandan and Rwandan armies that prowled their land, seeking to conquer and control the Congo because of the country's national resources, especially mineral riches.

"The village in which we met had been the scene of a massacre just weeks earlier. The walls and roof of the church were pock-marked with bullet holes. The floor of the church had run red with blood as it served as a morgue for the countless men and women killed.

"Yet there was about these pastors a security, a contentment that is found only in those who know and love the Lord, obeying him to the fullest."

As I listened to Carl talk and looked at his pictures of my brothers in Christ, I was reminded again of the diverse character and situation of the church. I've never had to face a military checkpoint or an invading army or the death angel of malnutrition. Chuck and I hop in our car and drive our fifteen minutes to church whenever we want and with no more concern than being certain there's enough gas to get us there. A special conference? Our participation is limited only by our budget. Just yesterday we signed up to attend a weekend marriage seminar an hour's drive away. The date's on the calendar for next February, and our greatest difficulty will be deciding which clothes to take.

Yet God asks the same things of us well-provisioned American Christians as he does of the pastors in the Congo: commitment and obedience. He asks that our hearts belong to him and that our lives evidence that commitment through our obedience. He asks that regardless of the circumstances in which we find ourselves we agree with him that he and what he has provided are sufficient for his purposes for us.

He asks for it all, even when we don't see his footprints before us, but he gives in return more than we could ever ask or think. He gives abundant life. "And God is able to make *all* grace abound to you, so that in *all* things at *all* times, *having all that you need,* you will abound in every good work" (2 Cor. 9:8, italics mine).

QUESTIONS, QUESTIONS

1. Read Proverbs 3:21–26. How does this type of planning differ from Rebekah's planning about Jacob and Esau?
2. Read Romans 3:20–24. What did trying to obey the Law accomplish? Can we earn God's favor and salvation by obeying? Why or why not?
3. If being obedient to God doesn't earn us eternity, why should we bother? Read Romans 11:33–12:2.
4. Read Ephesians 4:25–5:4. List all the commands, both positive and negative. What do these verses say about our feelings and emotions in regard to obedience? What conclusion can you draw from this?
5. Read Proverbs 14:1. Which woman are you? How are you modeling contentment in your home? Before your children? At work?
6. Which of the enemies of contentment that we've discussed in this book gives you the most difficulty? What ideas have you gotten that will help you deal with this area in a godly manner?

Notes

CHAPTER 2

1. Jerry Jenkins, "Fun Junkies, Beware," *Moody Monthly*, January 1987, 8.

CHAPTER 3

1. Charles Krauthammer, "Beware the Study of Turtles," *Time*, 28 June 1993, 76.

CHAPTER 4

1. Edward C. Knippers, Jr., "Hellfire of the Banalities," *Christianity Today*, 22 September 1989, 26.
2. Ibid.
3. Robert Benson, *Between the Dreaming and the Coming True* (New York: HarperCollins, 1996), 16–17.
4 Ibid., 24–25.
5. Larry Crabb, "A Fish in the Desert," *Moody Magazine*, July/August 1991, 32.
6. Ibid.

CHAPTER 5

1. Robert Fulghum, "Sigmund Wollman's Reality Test," as condensed in *Reader's Digest*, December 1993, 51–52, from Robert Fulghum, *Uh-Oh* (New York: Ivy Books, 1991), 145–46.

CHAPTER 6

1. Jan Johnson, *Madame Guyon* (Bloomington, Minn.: Bethany House, 1998), 43–44.
2. Lewis B. Smedes, *How Can It Be All Right When Everything Is All Wrong?* (Wheaton, Ill.: Harold Shaw, 1999), 54.

CHAPTER 7

1. Charles Swindoll, *The Grace Awakening* (Nashville, Tenn.: Word, 1996), 155.
2. Ibid., 155–56.
3. Gayle Roper, *Who Cares?* (Wheaton, Ill.: Harold Shaw, 1992), 42.

CHAPTER 8

1. Augustine, *The Confessions of St. Augustine,* quoted in "Reflections," *Christianity Today,* 23 November 1992.
2. Donald Kraybill, *The Puzzles of Amish Life* (Intercourse, Penn.: Good Books, 1995), 24–25.
3 Ibid., 26.
4. Alexander Solzhenitsyn, *Gulag Archipelago II* (New York: Harper & Row, 1974), 613–15, as quoted in Charles Colson, *Loving God* (Grand Rapids, Mich.: Zondervan, 1983), 35.

CHAPTER 9

1. Forrest Wilson, *Crusade in Crinoline* (Philadelphia, Penn.: J. B. Lippincott, 1941), 174.
2. Jan Johnson, *Madame Guyon* (Bloomington, Minn.: Bethany House, 1998), 49.

Chapter 10

1. J. Oswald Sanders, *Lonely but Never Alone* (Grand Rapids, Mich.: Discovery House), 16.
2. Larry Crabb and Dan Allender, *Encouragement* (Grand Rapids, Mich.: Zondervan, 1990), 112.
3. Ibid., 113.
4. Joni Eareckson Tada and Steven Estes, *When God Weeps* (Grand Rapids, Mich.: Zondervan, 1997), 128.

Chapter 11

1. J. I. Packer, *Knowing God* (Downers Grove, Ill.: InterVarsity, 1993), 18.

Chapter 12

1. Charles D. Kelley, "The Miracle of Contentment," *Discipleship Journal*, November/December 1997, as found in *Discipleship Journal CD Anthology* (Oak Harbor, Wash.: Logos Library System, Logos Research System, 1999).

Chapter 13

1. Charles Colson, *Loving God* (Grand Rapids, Mich.: Zondervan Publishing House, 1983), 36.
2. *The Best of A. W. Tozer*, Warren Wiersbe, compiler (Grand Rapids, Mich.: Baker, 1978), 114.
3. Charles D. Kelley, "The Miracle of Contentment," *Discipleship Journal*, November/December 1997, as found in *Discipleship Journal CD Anthology* (Oak Harbor, Wash.: Logos Library System, Logos Research System, 1999).
4. See Winifred Green and Gayle Roper, *Into Africa* (Camp Hill, Penn.: Horizon Books, 1995).